TOWARD A LOGIC OF MEANINGS

STATEMENT OF SPONSORSHIP

In an endeavor to promote easier access to and better understanding of Piaget's ideas by English-speaking scholars, the **Jean Piaget Society** and the **Foundation Archives Jean Piaget** encourage translations of important works not yet translated, support retranslations of inadequately translated texts, foster consistent translation of technical terms, and provide translators with expert consultation. This translation of Jean Piaget and Rolando Garcia's *Vers une logique des significations* reflects the efforts of these scholarly organizations.

JEAN PIAGET
ROLANDO GARCIA

TOWARD A LOGIC
OF MEANINGS

With the Collaboration of

L. Banks, I. Berthoud, D. de Caprona, S. Dionnet, J. Guyon, A. Henriques,
V. Jacq, H. Kilcher, D. Maurice, G. Merzaghi, C. Monnier, G. Piéraut-Le
Bonniec, E. Rappe du Cher, A. Ritter, A. Sinclair, C. Vachta, B. Vitale, A.
Wells, M. Zinder, and R. Zubel

Preface by Bärbel Inhelder
Edited by Philip M. Davidson & Jack Easley

BF
463
.M4
P53

LEA LAWRENCE ERLBAUM ASSOCIATES, PUBLISHERS
1991 Hillsdale, New Jersey   Hove and London

Lawrence Erlbaum Associates, Inc., Publishers
365 Broadway
Hillsdale, New Jersey 07642

Library of Congress Cataloging-in-Publication Data

Piaget Jean, 1896-
    Toward a logic of meanings / Jean Piaget, Rolando Garcia ; with the collaboration of L. Banks . . .
[et al.] ; preface by Barbel Inhelder ; edited by Phillip M. Davidson & Jack Easley.
        p.   cm.
    Includes bibliographical references and index.
    ISBN 0-8058-0301-7
    1. Meaning (Psychology) 2. Logic. 3. Knowledge, Theory of.
I. Garcia, Rolando. II. Banks, L. III. Davidson, Philip Minor. IV. Easley, J.A. V. Title.
BF463.M4P53 1991
153.4'3--dc20
                                                                                            91-12701
                                                                                                 CIP

Printed in the United States of America
10 9 8 7 6 5 4 3 2 1

CONTENTS

PREFACE

It seems to me that the importance of this book is that it responds both to current concerns with meaning and representation in psychology, and to a renewed interest of contemporary logic in the issue of relevance. The book is an account of investigations that Jean Piaget elaborated and carried out with his collaborators at the International Center for Genetic Epistemology in 1978-79. It is the very last book Piaget wrote.

Both the completion of a whole series of works and the opening of a new perspective, this volume attempts to recast operatory logic by extending it in two directions: towards the construction of a logic of meanings, from which operatory logic would naturally arise, and towards a new formulation of propositional logic, which has previously been too tightly linked to extensional logic.

As in *Psychogenesis and the History of Science*,[1] Jean Piaget's collaboration with Rolando Garcia proved fruitful from the very beginning of this experimental and theoretical investigation. Through intensive exchanges of ideas, notes and memos, the authors interacted at all stages in elaborating the conceptual framework of the research. Piaget concentrated throughout on a theory of meaning in natural logic, which Garcia enriched with his deep knowledge of contemporary logical theories.

The book is divided into two parts. Part I includes Piaget's text, which he had hoped to complete by integrating it with Garcia's results. As he himself unfortunately did not have time for such a synthesis, Garcia carried it out in his "General Conclusions."

Piaget intended to bring to light the very roots of logic by going back to implications between sensorimotor actions. Such a logic could only be a logic of meanings where implications are not restricted to statements: in the subject's view, every action or operation is endowed with meanings; therefore, one may deal with systems of implications among the meanings of actions, and then among the meanings of operations. Provided that the meaning of actions and the causality of actions are carefully distinguished, the subject's expectations and anticipations about the chaining of actions bear witness to the existence of early inferences. Hence a privileged form of inference is the action implication, which is an implication between the

---

[1]Piaget, J., & Garcia, R. *Psychogenesis and the History of Science*. (H. Feider, trans.). New York: Columbia University Press, 1989. (Original work published 1983)

meanings of actions. Piaget was thus initiating research on a "protologic" in which forms and contents are less differentiated than in operatory systems. After his investigations of correspondences,[2] elementary dialectics,[3] and categorial logic,[4] in which he brought out the elementary and formative stages of operations, Piaget was deepening his study of modes of understanding that are used as cognitive tools well before the subject can thematize them.

In Part II of the book, Garcia highlights Piaget's original contribution to the logic of meanings, a contribution that will be fully understood only within the framework of genetic epistemology. In the chapter titled "Logic and Genetic Epistemology," Garcia stresses that Piaget's purpose was not primarily to make a contribution to logic as such, but to develop a method of epistemological analysis. We hope this will dispel the all too frequent misunderstandings of certain formalizations that Piaget has proposed for analyzing the norms of rationality at all developmental levels.

When reading the chapter "Extensional Logic and Intensional Logic," nonspecialists will be grateful to Garcia for acquainting them with Anderson and Belnap's work on relevance and necessity in logic and for stating with great clarity the similarities and differences between operatory logic and the logic of relevance. Garcia views the latter as a necessary substratum for the former, and is the first to show how fruitful the joint study of both these logics can be.

Finally, in his "General Conclusions," which illuminate the whole work, Garcia gives a masterful interpretation of all the new discoveries in the book. He emphasizes a finding that seemingly contradicts what we had concluded from earlier studies: the early formation, at the level of actions and in the context of meanings, of operations that, although not yet integrated into structured wholes, are isomorphic to the 16 binary operations of propositional logic. These fragments of structures become progressively coordinated, eventually constituting the groupings and finally the *INRC* group. In this respect, let us notice that Garcia ascribes a dual attributive and integrative function to the process of assimilation,

[2]Piaget, J. *Recherches sur les correspondances.* (*Etudes d'Epistémologie Génétique*, vol. 37.) Paris: P.U.F., 1980.

[3]Piaget, J. *Les formes élémentaires de la dialectique.* Paris: Gallimard, 1980.

[4]Piaget, J.; in collaboration with G. Henriques and E. Ascher. *Morphisms and Categories: To Compare and Transform.* (T. Brown, trans.). Hillsdale, NJ: Lawrence Erlbaum Associates, in press.

thereby showing that a logic of meanings underlying the logic of statements must be both intensional and extensional.

Far from ending debates, this book opens new perspectives. We agree with Garcia's vision of a fully scientific and therefore modifiable epistemology, which alone can deal with and renew a classical issue like the problem of meaning. Moreover, the analysis allows a better understanding of the logic of actions and the various phenomena linked to an attribution of meanings in the child's cognitive activity. Broad areas of psychology are concerned with the intentions, goals and meaningful representations underlying cognitive behaviors. This book will certainly contribute to such questions, through the typical Piagetian interdisciplinary approach that has proved so fruitful in the past, and which will make the book of interest to logicians, epistemologists, psychologists, and all researchers who are receptive to new approaches to meaning.

We cordially thank our colleague J. B. Grize for his careful reading of the parts of Piaget's manuscript dealing with logic, and P. M. Davidson and J. Easley for their remarkable edition of the English translation. We also thank E. Ferreiro and S. Dionnet for editing the experimental parts, D. de Caprona and P. M. Davidson for translating Part I of the book into English, P. Steenken for the artwork and all the collaborators at the International Center for Genetic Epistemology and the Jean Piaget Archives Foundation. Once again, the research and writing were possible thanks to subsidies from the Swiss National Fund for Scientific Research, the Ford Foundation and the Jean Piaget Foundation for Psychological and Epistemological Research.

Bärbel Inhelder

EDITORS' COMMENTS

The first two sentences of Piaget's Introduction to this book refer to operatory logic and logical intension. A few preliminary remarks about these concepts may be in order, especially since Piaget's proposals about operatory logic have been misunderstood in the past.

Inhelder and Piaget's books on logical thinking[1] have been criticized by logicians for their use of logic and their claims about children's logical abilities. Papert[2] put it well when he wrote, "What the logicians reproach Piaget for is often just what he has done best," namely to invent a new use for logical ideas originally developed for other purposes. He notes that there is really no choice in starting a new field—one has to use existing instruments that were developed for other fields. Instead of considering logic as rules of valid inference or as a method of systematically avoiding misleading and invalid reasoning, Piaget has used its notation and some of its concepts instead to make a model[3] for describing children's intellectual development, which progresses through stages of what is often technically illogical reasoning. This serves his major epistemological purpose, largely ignored by logicians, to explain how logical reasoning—especially respecting number, geometry, and parts of physics—has arisen conceptually, step-by-step, out of actions. Another way of viewing Piaget's operatory logic is to notice that in the clinical interviews which provide the basic data of his research, children often use logical forms to suggest new ways of thinking about a problem: they use them heuristically, not only for deductively testing the validity of inferences, as in the formal application of logic.

In the present volume Piaget and Garcia expand and revise the earlier work on operatory logic by analyzing meaning relations in clinical interviews and by incorporating a logic of intensions (derived by Anderson

---

[1]Inhelder, B., & Piaget, J. *The Early Growth of Logic: Classification and Seriation.* New York: Harper & Row, 1964; and *The Growth of Logical Thinking: From Childhood to Adolescence.* New York: Basic Books, 1958.

[2]Papert, S. "Sur la logique Piagétienne," in *La filiation des structures. (Etudes d'Epistémologie Génétique,* No. 15.) Paris: P.U.F., 1963.

[3]See Piaget's *Essai de logique opératoire.* (Paris: Dunod, 1972). The general idea is sketched in Piaget's *Logic and Psychology,* Manchester University Press, 1953.

and Belnap[4] from the work on natural deduction by Gentzen and many others).

Webster's Second International Dictionary (1950) gives the following definition of "intension" in the field of logic: "The sum of the attributes, qualities, or marks comprised in a concept or implied in a term; the essence, content, or connotation; thus the 'intension' of triangle implies or includes that of 'plane figure'." Webster's Third New International Dictionary (1970) adds, "contrasted with extension." To assess all the meanings Webster alludes to, one might have to read a lot of philosophy. For example, the Schilpp volume on Rudolf Carnap[5] contains articles by six somewhat similarly oriented philosophers dealing with the intension-extension distinction and Carnap's replies to them. Readers who are interested in the logical issues raised by the present volume can turn to a number of other helpful sources as well.[6]

A further comment is in order for readers who are familiar with Piaget's use of the intension-extension distinction in previous writings. For instance, in their work on early logic, Inhelder and Piaget (1964)[1] studied children's differentiation of a class's intension from its extension. And Piaget has consistently characterized the comparison of a whole with its part as "intensive" quantification[7] because it involves qualitative reasoning, as contrasted with the numerical reasoning required in comparing two sets of elements. Thus, these previous usages pertain to children's

[4]Anderson, A. R., & Belnap, N. D. Entailment: The Logic of Relevance and Necessity. Princeton: Princeton University Press, 1975.

[5]Schilpp, P. A. The Philosophy of Rudolf Carnap. La Salle, IL: Open Court, 1963.

[6]See, for example, Berlin, I., "Logical Translation" in H. Hardy (Ed.), Concepts and Categories—Philosophical Essays. New York: Viking Press, 1979; Carnap, R., Introduction to Symbolic Logic and its Applications, (pp. 39-42, 98-100). New York: Dover Publications, 1958; Goddard, L., & Routley, R. The Logic of Significance and Context. Edinburgh: Scottish Academic Press, 1973, (Chapter 7); Haack, S. Philosophy of Logics. Cambridge University Press, 1978, (pp. 175-203); Quine, W. V. O. Word and Object—an Inquiry into the Linguistic Mechanisms of Objective Reference. Cambridge, MA: The Technology Press & Wiley, 1960, (pp. 164ff, pp. 212ff); Van Benthem, J. A Manual of Intensional Logic. Stanford, CA: Center for the Study of Language and Information, 1988; Zalta, E. N. Intensional Logic and the Metaphysics of Intentionality. Cambridge, MA: MIT Press, 1988; and of course Anderson, A. R., & Belnap, N. D., op. cit.

acquisition of specific concepts, or their application of specific forms of reasoning. In contrast, the present usage pertains to the foundations of thought itself, inasmuch as Piaget proposes relevance and intension as the basis for natural deduction.

The central problem for the present project is to uncover the origins of relevance as a relation between intensions, and the role of relevance in the development of natural logic. Piaget shows, in Chapter 1, how a hook is relevant to an infant for lifting a toy monkey with a coiled tail. Part of the meaning of a hook is that there are loops it can enter, thus supporting another object or fastening two objects together. Part of the meaning of the monkey's coiled tail is that it can fasten the monkey to some support. The intensions of the two objects are relevant to each other and to the intention of the child wanting the toy. Garcia then shows how Anderson & Belnap's logic of entailment can be adapted to Piaget's analysis of children's behavior.

Piaget wrote in 1980, the year in which he died, "Our more recent work...on the notions of possibility and necessity followed by that on the construction of a logic of meanings, provides still clearer arguments in favor of a constructivist theory and its explanation of the elaboration of new concepts and operations."[8] Among these arguments is that the logic of meanings is a natural instrument for describing "augmentative" equilibrations, those leading to enriched constructions: "At all levels of development there are implications between actions or meanings; then there are dialectical relations that lead the subject to go beyond what he has already acquired."[8] Equally important is that the intensional formulation avoids the paradoxes of extensional logic and material implication, according to which "p implies q whatever the relationship between p and q may be and without there being any link between their meanings."[8]

In editing this volume we have at times been startled by the shift of perspective required in thinking intensionally rather than extensionally about certain familiar contexts. For instance, when Piaget says that the number of possible second elements in counting around a circle of buttons

[7]Piaget, J., & Inhelder, B. *The Child's Construction of Quantities: Conservation and Atomism.* London: Routledge & Kegan Paul, 1975, pp. 18-21.

[8]Piaget, J. "Recent Studies in Genetic Epistemology," in *Cahiers de la fondation archives Jean Piaget,* No. 1. Genève: Fondation Archives Jean Piaget, 1980, pp. 3-7.

is *twice* the number of buttons—because of the two possible directions of counting—he is thinking of "second element" as an intension that is distinct from its literal extension. Readers may have experienced similar puzzlement on first encountering various well-known intensional definitions ("morning star" does not mean the same thing as "evening star"; the intension of "equiangular triangles" differs from that of "equilateral triangles").

As a teacher educator, one of us (J.E.) notes that schooling, especially in mathematics, often involves an effort to eradicate intensional in favor of extensional reasoning. One side effect may be the widespread reduction of mathematics to meaningless computation for both teachers and their pupils. In any case, it is clear that one's prior training may either help or hinder one's assimilation of this final articulation of Piaget's operatory logic. Fortunately, Piaget follows his usual format, exploring the development of children's meaning inferences from a variety of angles until the pattern is inescapable. We have nevertheless added footnotes where the text is less clear, which we hope will be of value to at least some readers.

P. M. Davidson and Jack Easley, Editors

PART ONE
by
Jean Piaget

Translated by D. de Caprona and P. M. Davidson

INTRODUCTION

Our main purpose in this book is to complete and to amend our operatory logic in the direction of a logic of meanings. It is already such a logic in the extensional sense of the term, and it is therefore in the intensional sense that we shall have to specify the use of logical connectives such as "and" and "or," and, above all, the use of "meaning implications" as opposed to "material implications." The difference between the two types of implications is that the latter are defined with respect to the truth values of statements, irrespective of their meanings or the meaning of the relation between them. Thus, considering only extensions, it suffices that any one term of the disjunction

$$(p \cdot q) \vee (\overline{p} \cdot q) \vee (\overline{p} \cdot \overline{q})$$

be true in order to derive the implication $p \supset q$ — even if there is no meaningful relation between p and q. This is the source of several well known paradoxes.[1]

Therefore, it is essential to construct a logic of meanings whose major operation we shall call a "meaning implication": p implies q (written $p \rightarrow q$) if one meaning m of q is embedded in the meanings of p and if this meaning m is transitive.[2] In this case, the embeddings of various meanings according to their relative comprehensiveness—which we shall call "inherences," correspond to extensional nestings, and therefore to kinds of truth tables. However, such truth tables are partial and are determined by meanings, and negations are relativized according to these nestings taken as frames of reference.[3]

---

[1]The paradoxes of material implication, which derive from the fact that p materially implies q if either p is false or q is true, include the following theorems: $p \rightarrow (q \rightarrow p)$; $p \rightarrow (\overline{p} \rightarrow q)$; and $(p \rightarrow q) \vee (q \rightarrow p)$. For discussions, see Anderson, A. R., & Belnap, N. D., *Entailment: The Logic of Relevance and Necessity*, Princeton: Princeton University Press, 1975, pp. 3-17; Haack, S. *Philosophy of Logics*, Cambridge: Cambridge University Press, 1978, pp. 176-203. (P.M.D.)

[2]Since transitivity is a property of relations, it would seem that this refers to the relation of sharing meaning. Thus, to say a meaning m is transitive means that if r shares m with q, and q shares m with p, then r shares m with p. The point is clarified somewhat by Piaget in "Recent Studies in Genetic Epistemology," *Cahiers de la Fondation Archives Jean Piaget*, No. 1, 1980, p. 5. (P.M.D.)

[3]This means, e.g., since the class of squares is included in the class of rectangles, if s = "this figure is a square," then $\overline{s}$ — that "this figure is not a square"—does

If such a logic of meanings really exists, there is no reason why it should be limited to propositions or statements, for any action or operation also has meanings. As no action, no operation, and above all no meaning is isolated but is bound up with many others, there are implications among the meanings of actions or of operations. Such implications are distinct although inseparable from the causal aspect, or the actual execution, of actions.

Our second purpose therefore is to advance the analysis of implications between actions or operations, by going back as far as possible to the level of practical action and in the direction of the most elementary inferences. At the level of true operations (around six to ten years), the analysis is straightforward. For instance, an operation that combines objects x into a class obviously implies an exclusion of objects y (or non-x). As Spinoza said, *omnis determinatio est negatio*. But with respect to practical actions, we must distinguish their causal aspect (the outcome that is verifiable after the fact) from their anticipation, which is inferential. An action in itself is neither true nor false, and is evaluated only in terms of effectiveness or usefulness in relation to a goal. Whereas, an action implication involving anticipations is either true or false and therefore already constitutes a logic, even at the most primitive levels. In addition, because meanings ensue from the assimilation of objects to the subject's schemes, and reciprocally, all assimilations engender meanings, a causal

not mean that it is anything at all, but only that it is not a rectangle.
[It would seem that the last three words "not a rectangle" might have been intended to read "a non-equilateral rectangle." In this simple case involving two intensions, squareness (s) is relativised to rectangularity (r) and we obtain the following "partial" truth table:

s	r	$\bar{s}$	$s \to r$
T	T	F	T
T	F	F	F
F	T	T	x
F	F	T	y

The value of x is true and y is false under the present interpretation (s = "non-equilateral rectangle," which shares meaning with "rectangle") whereas x and y are both true regardless of shared meaning under the extensional interpretation. (P.M.D.)]

succession of observable events is a sufficient condition for implications between meanings. For example, an object x might be laid on a support y which the subject could use to draw it back, or else it might be placed next to the support. Observing either situation brings out implications between meanings, as long as the subject understands that in the latter case it is useless to pull at the support: the relation or action "laying down upon" has acquired the meaning of a "reason."

From this standpoint, various levels can be distinguished. The most elementary one consists in constructing action, object, and relation schemes in the midst of the global perceptual images that comprise the newborn infant's world. In this initially undifferentiated universe, any change at first merely amounts to substituting one global picture for a previous one, without any detailed analysis of possible modifications. Starting with this essentially syncretic situation, the first cognitive endeavors are tantamount to carving out a number of relatively isolable and stable elements through repeatable actions (the origin of action schemes). Thus, objects and relations are formed, serving as content for inferences or implications between meanings and actions.

We have previously described the arduous and rather late (age 10-12 months) conquest of object permanence under various conditions in which the object is screened.[4] Since then, many works (by Bower[5] and others) have shown that this construction is even more complex than in our description. Recent studies[6] describe other schemes that are elaborated around 9-10 months. Faced with empty cubes of various sizes, with sticks and small balls of plasticine, some subjects show an intention to insert a smaller cube in a bigger one but, interestingly enough, instead of directly doing so, they first put it in their mouth: They construct the container-content scheme (in the present case, a relation), through a form of "reflective abstraction," from the routine and well established scheme of "putting something into one's mouth." They then extend it to new, somewhat intercoordinated schemes or sub-schemes such as to insert and to take out, to fill and to empty, or to iterate the inserting action so that a cube which is a "content" becomes a "container" for a smaller cube. The

[4]Piaget, J. *The Origins of Intelligence in Children.* New York: Norton, 1963.
[5]Bower, T. G. R. *Development in Infancy.* San Francisco: Freeman, 1974.
[6]Sinclair, H., Stambak, M., Lezine, I., Rayna, S., & Verba, M. *Les bébés et les choses.* Paris: Presses Universitaires de France, 1982.

balls, cubes and sticks will eventually all be used as contents and the six cubes as containers.

As for the balls of plasticine, babies will stick two or more together in order to constitute a continuous whole, then separate them to restore the previous discontinuous state. Other objects, sticks for instance, will be used for hitting, throwing, pushing, and so on. These facts are interesting in that they show the construction of relational schemes which may be intercoordinated, especially when a positive action (such as inserting, etc.) is followed by the reverse action (taking out, emptying, etc.). This comprises the beginning of implications among actions, such as "action x implies the possibility of the reverse action." Various processes such as differentiation of actions, individualization and localization of objects, clustering, elementary classifying activities, correspondences, and so on, can also be observed.

We may call this initial level a "protological" one, understanding by this a preparatory phase leading to the instruments for deduction proper. This phase is marked by the formation and coordination of the first assimilation schemes, and therefore of the first meaning implications (for instance, when relations are established between vision and grasping through a progressive evaluation of accurate distances).

This initial phase is followed by another level, still characterized by sensorimotor implications among actions, which in this case are sufficiently systematic to engender stable structures. For instance, once object permanence is elaborated with respect to objects temporarily hidden by a screen, the subject will discover that they occupy the last of their successive positions and not the first one. This implies that positions and displacements are co-ordinated, and therefore that the "group of displacements"[7] is being formed. Needless to say, such structurations require not only the constitution of positive implications, but also an adequate use of exclusions or negations, in addition to the above-mentioned initial inversions.

When the semiotic function is being elaborated, action implications are accompanied by verbal expressions, leading to meaning implications among statements. Such implications are still determined by meanings and cannot be reduced to extensions, as they remain dependent upon nestings and inherences lacking a general truth table.

[7]Piaget, J. op. cit., pp. 241-247.

At this level, our studies yield a third interesting outcome: We observe the formation of rudimentary operations in action contexts, each of which is isomorphic to one of the sixteen binary operations of propositional logic. Naturally, these precursory operations are isolated and related to specific meanings, rather than being organized into structured wholes (such as groupings, etc.). We formerly considered such operations as characteristic of systems that are elaborated around age 11-12, and had two reasons for thinking so. First, this period marks the beginning of hypothetico-deductive thought, the capacity to infer necessary consequences from sheer hypotheses, without depending on data (as at the level of "concrete operations," around 7-10 years). The second reason for supposing a late development is that at the hypothetico-deductive level, these 16 operations arise as a system of relations between inverses (N) and reciprocities (R) constituting quaternality groups (the $INRC$ groups in which C is the inverse of R and the correlative of identity I).[8] These groups are used for example in solving problems of physics, such as those involving the equality of actions and reactions. Therefore, it is both striking and instructive to rediscover the 16 operations at the level of the coordinations among actions, well before deductive thinking and *a fortiori* well before *INRC* structures are used.

What we actually observe at early levels are the 16 possible ways of combining pairs of actions, without systematic interrelations, in which each combination is performed according to context. Moreover, as the logical connectives "and" or "or" have various intensional meanings that we wish to distinguish, the 16 types of combinations involve much more than 16 distinct operations, according as subjects elaborate various forms of conjunctions, disjunctions, incompatibilities, or other combinations in particular situations on the basis of meaning implications. Whether implicit or explicit, these implications may be reduced theoretically (i.e., from the observer's standpoint) to combinations of implications and negations: for instance, $p \circ q$ (where the intensional conjunction $\circ$ $=_{Df} \bar{p} \to q$) and $p \vee q$ (where the intensional disjunction $\vee =_{Df} \overline{p \to \bar{q}}$). This amounts to asserting that at all levels, the foundation of all logic is of an inferential nature, which is natural in the case of a logic of meanings.

---

[8]Piaget, J. *Essai de logique opératoire* (J.B. Grize, ed.). (Second edition of the *Traité de logique*, 1949). Paris: Dunod, 1971. [The statements in parentheses can be read $C = NR$ & $C = CI$. (P.M.D.)]

In a word, the purpose of this book is to reveal the construction of such a logic; this constitutes a natural and necessary extension of our operatory logic that was until now too closely (although only partially) linked to the more familiar extensional logic. The reader might feel that this goal actually involves two specific projects that are so different that they should have been pursued in two separate parts of the book to avoid possible confusions. The first would be to describe the formation and multiplication of meanings, stressing both their diversity and their shared features, and thus examining "the meaning of meanings" (see Ogden and Richard's well known book, *The Meaning of Meaning*).[9] The second would be a close analysis of meaning implications, especially those consisting of implications between actions or operations (and which, if we are not mistaken, hardly anyone else has discussed).

The two endeavors are distinct and we may give the impression of unnecessarily mixing them. However, in spite of their differences, they cannot be dissociated for an essential reason that we must stress from the outset: Their unity lies not only in some shared features (related, for instance, through an inclusion or intersection), but in the much more important and instructive fact that they actually are two terms in a dialectical relation, and therefore two poles in a cycle that prevails from the outset and grows as a spiral throughout development.

As was mentioned above, any observable is always linked to an interpretation which necessarily involves not only meanings, but also inferential links between these meanings or to previous meanings. Such inferences, whether explicit or implicit, from their earliest forms can only consist of implications between meanings, and therefore between action schemes. Thus, even the most elementary scheme, the preformed sucking reflex, already involves implications (between displacements and successes or failures, i.e., when the newborn must change its position in order to adjust its ill-positioned mouth to the nipple). As for entirely acquired behavior, we shall see in chapter I how meanings and implications are simultaneously elaborated through the use of tools.

[9]Ogden, C., & Richards, I. A. *The Meaning of Meaning*, 4th ed. London: Routledge, 1936.

1

MEANINGS AND IMPLICATIONS IN
INSTRUMENTAL BEHAVIOR

With D. de Caprona and A. Ritter

This study analyzes the formation of meanings and action implications in the behavior that has been so often and so well studied since W. Köhler's work on chimpanzees: the use of various objects as "instruments" to reach what the hand cannot. We take up this classical problem because this behavior has seldom been analyzed from the viewpoint of its internal logic, a logic that ensures the transition from sensorimotor logic to that of preoperatory anticipations and representations.

The apparatus [Figure 1] consists of a wide board at the end of which three objects are displayed in a row: (1) On the left is a stuffed monkey in a fixed, transparent box; the box is closed on all sides but open on top, so one can lift the monkey out by hooking its tail; (2) On the right is a dog in a similar box open on one side and on the top; one can push the animal through the open side at the back of the box, make it go around the box and pull it to oneself; (3) There is no box in between, but a cat, which can simply be pulled. The following tools are freely available: (1) A stick, 35 cm long; (2) Another stick, 40 cm long, with a hook on the end with which to lift the monkey or to push the dog; (3) A rake, 35 cm long; and (4) An angled stick, 35 cm long, whose bend may be used to push the dog or to pull the dog and the cat. Older subjects are presented with straight connectible sections, 15 cm in length, which may be used to modify tools (1) to (4).

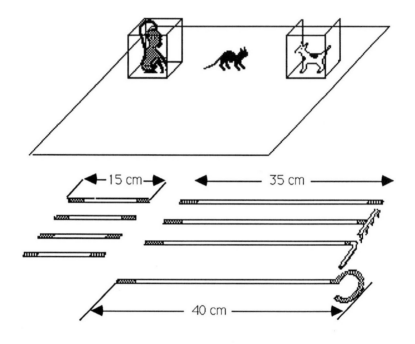

Figure 1.

Three levels may be distinguished in the reactions observed. The first level is characterized by mere exploration, aimed at attributing meanings to the four potential mediators, but limited to immediate manipulations such as hitting, pushing, and so forth. The subjects don't conceive of these mediators as tools for retrieving the desired objects, and therefore don't use them as instruments. This non-instrumental level is followed by an intermediate level (level II) in which instrumental meanings first appear, although they remain sporadic and mixed with level I behaviors. Finally, at level III, instrumental behaviors are acquired either through immediate success or through more or less laborious efforts.

1. Level I

First of all, here are some examples from *level I*:

SOA (1;2). Despite an instruction to "go get" the animals with the tools, *Soa* shows no interest in the tools and only makes unsuccessful bids at grasping throughout the session. When the rake is placed before the cat, she gathers the sticks and pushes them toward the cat, making it fall off the board. She does likewise with the dog's box, which doesn't move. The cat is put back in its initial position and once again she pushes it gradually until it falls off. She looks at the cat, then at her hand, while moving her fingers (thus showing her desire to grasp the cat); then she reaches toward the cat, but without trying to make contact with the stick which she has placed just beside her outstretched arm.

XAN (1;8) tries to get closer to the cat in order to grasp it. Still looking at the cat, he puts the rake on top of the board and hits it without any pulling action. This behavior is repeated several times during the session either with the rake only, or with all the tools held together. Then he takes the rake by its tines, turns it upside down, changes hands, hits the board once again, slides the hook back and forth, picks up the angled stick, looks at the bend, lays it down on the board, and so on. The experimenter pulls in the cat with the rake and then puts it back where it was; *Xan* imitates this behavior but makes no use of it thereafter. When the demonstration is repeated with the stick, he picks up the rake and, instead of aiming at the cat, uses it to hit the board repeatedly. He takes the angled stick, holds it at the bend, inserts the other end in one of the boxes and pushes it instead of trying to pull. He inserts the end of the rake in the dog's box and then hits the board, first with the rake, then with the angled stick. He also repeats these behaviors with several tools held together.

CHI (1;1) picks up the rake and uses it to sweep from side to side, rake, rub, and finally to hit the board. When the experimenter points to the cat that is to be retrieved (repeating the instruction several times), the child places the end of the rake in front of the cat, pushing it forward three times. Next he holds the rake vertically and hits the board, and does the same thing with the hook. When he is shown the dog out of the box with the rake pointing to it, he takes the rake, licks it, points to the dog with his finger, then leans forward and grasps it with his hand. The same behavior is observed with the stick.

BEL (1;4). Despite the instructions, *Bel* initially explores the tools without relating them to the animals. He picks up the rake and the hook and moves them several times, rolls the stick on the table or holds it up, all the while observing the animals. Shown how to pull back the cat with the stick, the child takes the hook but pushes the cat instead of pulling it toward him. The experimenter pulls the cat with the rake, but *Bel* imitates this action only insofar as he pulls the rake, without contacting the animal or even looking at it. The experimenter performs the action once again: This time the child touches the cat with the rake, but he pushes it away until it falls off the board. When the cat is put back in its initial position, the child resumes his efforts with lateral movements, unintentionally hitting the monkey's box. As for the dog, he limits himself to hitting it and the box, then he likewise hits the board and the cat. Finally, he tries without avail to hook the monkey, which represents a first instrumental relation, although an abortive one. When retested two months later, *Bel* reaches level II (see below).

PAO (1;9) is interesting because she connects the tools and the animals but without using the former to pull the latter. First she picks up the stick, looks at it and lays it down. Given the rake, she looks at it, turns it, puts it on the board, pushes it but stops short of touching the cat. The cat is placed half-way: Now she touches the cat, but then reverts to direct grasping instead of using the tool. Once again the cat is placed half-way: Although she puts the rake on the back of the animal, she finally clutches it with her hand. The experimenter demonstrates pulling the cat with the rake, and then hands the rake to the child. After having held it up to investigate its form, she balances it vertically on its teeth.

These initial reactions are interesting in several respects. First of all, they are clearly not at all instrumental as required by the instruction to fetch animals that are too distant to be grasped. In other words, the four potential intermediaries do not yet have the meaning of useful means for reaching the specified goal. Even when, as with *Bel*, the experimenter demonstrates pulling the cat with the rake so that the child may imitate what he has just seen, he has such a poor understanding of the relation "pulling with an instrument" that he makes no subsequent use of it and uses the rake only to hit the board. Neither is it as might be thought, that the subject forgets or ignores the instruction. For instance, *Soa* looks at the cat and at her hand while working her fingers, then moves her hand towards the cat but lays the stick parallel to her arm without trying to make contact. Thus, these children both understand what should be done and fail to understand the relations that would enable them to do it.

The significance of the observed behavior is equally fascinating. The initial phase of exploring the four tools must be conceived as a search for their meanings, in terms of "what can be done" with them. These meanings are of two kinds: some relate to the general properties of the tools, whereas more occasional ones bear on establishing possible relations with the animals. Included in meanings of the first type are that the stick may be laid down, rolled (*Bel*), or held vertically on the table; that the rake may be grasped by the handle or the tines, or be made to stand vertically; that it is possible to move or slide the tools, but impossible to deform them; and that they are equal in length yet different at their ends. Whereas these general meanings are ordinary and are noticed and recorded at once by older subjects, what we find interesting about the first level is that young subjects need active explorations before they notice them. This shows that meanings are the attributions of actions (i.e., assimilation schemes) to objects; thus object properties are not reducible to "pure" observables, where "pure" means without any form of interpretation.

As for the meanings that relate to the immediate situation—in this case animals that have to be reached—these are already numerous although none of them involves the idea of "pulling to oneself." The simplest of all is to move the intermediary toward the target, as *Soa* lays the stick parallel to her stretched arm, which shows an intention to bring the object nearer. Another behavior which is as frequent as this but whose meaning is less clear, is hitting the board. This might seem to involve a meaning of the first type, but it more likely indicates an intention to shake the animals, and therefore to dislodge them with the hope that they will get nearer (*Bel*, for instance, alternately hits the board and the cat). When an animal is touched by a tool, the two most prevalent maneuvers are to push the object or to shift it laterally, instead of pulling it. It is just as if the instrument were a continuation of the subject's arm—as a matter of fact, of the arm only and not both the arm and the hand as in grasping.

If, according to our guiding hypothesis, all these general and local meanings consist of attributions of actions to objects, what about the implications between meanings or actions? They are so implicit that one may be tempted to think they don't yet exist. But we doubt this because to attribute meanings either to objects or actions is to interpret them, and interpretation is a complex, fundamentally inferential behavior, however trivial its implications may be: To reach an object implies getting closer to it, and to push it implies continuing this "going toward" movement; whereas to pull back would imply a movement in the opposite direction, hence its greater difficulty. To sweep laterally implies a shift from the "toward" direction to its perpendicular; hitting the board implies that a positive outcome is possible; and so on. Briefly, every action takes place between a set of preliminary conditions and a set of certain or possible results. This accounts for the presence, at this very first level, of proactive and retroactive implications (Peirce's "predictive" and "retrodictive" implications).

2. Intermediate cases between "pushing" and "pulling"

At level I, one sometimes sees examples of lateral sweeping movements, but they are not intended or understood by the subject as a possible transition to a pulling motion. The following examples show how subjects use lateral movements to reach the solution.

BEL (1;6) (Retested two months after his level I reactions.) As in the first session, *Bel* starts by hitting the board, pushing the target and so on. However, after having placed the tines of the rake behind the cat, he gets the idea of moving the animal towards his other hand. He puts the rake on the cat's back, pulls it sideways and succeeds in taking it with his free hand. On the next trial, he intends to move the cat from the right toward the left hand, but he is unsuccessful in doing so. Once again, he puts the tines on the cat's back, presses hard and makes it turn, but he is unable to place the rake behind the cat and he simply pushes it. He then hits it repeatedly, which brings it a little nearer. After knocking one of the boxes, he pushes the whole board and hits on the idea of pulling it, enabling him to grasp the animal. Then using the hook he once again brings the cat closer to his free hand. Turning to the monkey, he inserts the hook in the box but fails to hook the monkey. As for the dog, he restricts himself to tapping the box.

CRI (2;2) starts by moving the cat laterally with the hook, then moves it with the rake and grabs it with the other hand. In contrast, he pulls the cat straight back when the experimenter places the rake behind it. He also succeeds in taking the dog out of the box, but only to clutch it manually.

JOE (2;10) places a tool behind the cat, pulls it a little toward him, then laterally, until he can take it with the other hand. But he succeeds in taking the monkey out of the box with the hook and pulls it all the way back. Afterwards he successfully retrieves the cat. The dog, however, once removed from its box, is only pulled a few centimeters until it can be seized by hand.

CAP (2;10). When asked, "Could you pull the cat with the rake?", she answers, *No*. She tries anyway and she succeeds in two motions. This success leads her to think that she could achieve the same result with the other animals and tools. The dog is placed in the middle of the board, outside its box. She first picks up the stick but says, *This one is for later on.* She selects the angled stick instead: *This one, yes*, and retrieves the dog. But she misses the monkey, as well as the dog when it is back in the box, by failing to differentiate the movements required within the boxes.

From the viewpoint of implications among actions, these transitional cases are instructive. In addition to hitting and pushing, level I subjects sometimes perform lateral sweeping movements, but without any intention of bringing the object closer. The present behaviors, in contrast, effect oblique displacements from the hand holding the tool to the free and waiting hand. Therefore, what we have here is a form of synthesis between instrumental maneuvers and manual grasping. Above all, what is involved is an inference that amounts to saying that if certain trajectories have been accomplished, others may be possible also. This leads a number of subjects to proceed from pushing to lateral or oblique movements, and eventually to drawing in the object. Furthermore, we may notice in *Cap* a tendency toward generalization: She intends to deal with the various animals with different tools (the stick is "for later on"), although she fails, except when she pulls the cat with the rake after denying that it was possible.

3. Levels II and III

We shall include in level II subjects who succeed at once in bringing back the cat but fail with the monkey and, above all, with the dog. Since those two are positioned in boxes, differentiations and coordinations of actions are required. Here are some examples:

ANO (3;4) pulls the cat right away with the rake which he has stretched out and brought down on the animal. As for the dog, he lays the hook on the upper edge of the box and pulls at it through the opening but eventually gives up. He puts the rake on one edge, inserts it in the box, pushing and pulling the whole apparatus while trying to take out the animal. He gives up. *Ano* then places the hook behind the monkey, and touches the end of the tail without paying attention to its curl. However, partly by chance, he succeeds in taking it out, but doesn't draw it to himself before clasping it with his hand.

ROL (3;6) places the rake over and then behind the cat and hauls it back. As for the dog, he doesn't push it out of the box but pulls on the box, turns the dog over, and so on, concluding, *The dog doesn't want to come.* He has another try with the angled stick and says: *I can't make it.* He tries the other tools, again turning over the dog, but without avail. He takes the monkey out of the box with the hook, which happened to drop into the loop of the tail (hence a localized shift to level III).

MAN (3;5) nudges the dog and turns it over five times, but never gets it out.

Here are examples from level III:

JES (2;1: precocious). *Jes* has no problem pulling the cat, and turns to the monkey with the rake. He places it under the animal, lifting it up a little, using the handle as a lever against the edge of the box. He does so five times until the monkey drops out of the box. The animal is put back into the box and *Jes* is asked to find another procedure. He uses the hook successfully, by inserting it in the loop of the tail. Afterwards, he uses the hook to push the dog through the open side of the box (opposite the subject) and to draw it back to him.

CAR (3;4). With the dog, he starts by levering it with the rake up along one side of the box, and he says: *We can do it this way.* When he notices that it is simpler to push it through the open rear side of the box, he pushes back the animal, shifts it to the left in two motions and draws it to him. He does likewise with the angled stick. Then he has fun lengthening the tools with the appropriate sections.

ROS (3;6) immediately hooks the tail of the monkey and pulls it to her. She selects the rake for the dog. She pushes it toward the back saying, *There is no door here*, and then attempts to pull the animal forward.

DAN (4;6). With the tines of the rake, she hooks the monkey through its tail and takes it out. For the dog, she first picks up the hook and only manages to turn the animal around. Then she takes the angled stick, thrusts the dog out of the box, and pulls it to her.

ANA (4;6) shows the same reactions: She immediately pushes the dog out behind the box, then to the left, and hauls it in. The monkey is very cautiously lifted up, with several brief pauses.

Only at level III are the three following schemes coordinated: to push the dog to make it go out behind the box; to move it laterally around the box; and to pull it back to oneself. We may thus assume that anticipations and a plan of action are involved which are still lacking at level II—where although the goals are clear enough, the means remain dependent upon trial-and-error behaviors, with partial successes or failures that are not always understood.

As far as meanings are concerned, we notice progress toward new meanings for objects or tools. These are no longer rigid, elongated, featureless solid objects handy for pulling whatever the hand cannot reach. At level III, each part of the instrument has a specific meaning: The meaning of the curve in the hook is to hook; the flat end of the angled stick has a meaning of pushing or pulling, as does the end of the rake, although the latter is wider. The stick is the only instrument with no specialized functional meaning.

The present study raises a basic problem about implications between actions that are characterized by their functional meaning, and one that we shall meet again in other studies: how to account for the distinction between causal relations and implicative inferences. Indeed, at each stage the sequence of actions obviously presents a causal aspect (and moreover a teleonomical one): To pull the dog back to oneself after taking it out of a box is a causal outcome (one of several possible) because the actions are chained, conditioned, and determined successively, rather than being a mere series of observables in the manner of Hume's regular successions. Therefore, beginning with the elementary sensorimotor forms studied in this chapter, we need to justify our constantly speaking of implications between the meanings of actions.

In the first place, we may argue that the subjects, depending on the level they have reached, may refrain from overt actions and confine themselves to anticipating everything they could actually do, including the errors that are to be avoided. To anticipate is to deduce, and any deduction or inference is a series or a system of implications.

A second argument is that such inferential anticipations do not bear on the material conditions of the actions (that is, on the detailed movements of the muscles of the acting arm or hand), but on meanings attributed by the subject's cognitive schemes. These attributions occur in any interpretation of objects and the activities performed on them.

Third, the plans that the subjects set for themselves are accompanied from the outset by justifications that successes or failures will later corroborate or invalidate. These justifications are different from, but preparatory to, truth values.

Finally, the coordination of the three schemes "to push out," "to move laterally," and "to pull to oneself," which characterizes level III (in the situation of the dog, where the box is open at the rear) is a deductive anticipation of a higher type, involving the construction of a complete scheme out of partial schemes that are coordinated by the whole. As an implication between implications, it is undeniable that this coordinating scheme is inferential in nature. Although it may be representational, surpassing the purely sensorimotor level, its constituents must have been previously prepared, and this entails the existence of simpler and more elementary implications.

Therefore, these reflections seem to allow us to use the notion of implications between actions, as distinct from their causation. Needless to say, causality is equally involved and, although different, these two aspects of instrumental behavior are inseparable. We can even go further and assert that the inferential systems involved here constitute "models," and that causal thought consists precisely in the attribution of these models to objects and their actions outside the subject. Otherwise, causality would be reduced to the regular succession of observables with which empiricists erroneously content themselves.

2

DISPLACEMENTS IN A TREE STRUCTURE

With C. Monnier and C. Vachta

In the previous chapter, children had to create paths for objects to follow. In the present situation, the paths are branch roads in the form of a tree and the children only have to choose among them. Such choices require inclusions and exclusions and, as a tree is isomorphic to a "grouping" of classes, the initial action implications (whether they are erroneous and have to be corrected or are right the first time) become gradually more intercoordinated from one developmental level to the next, until they end up as true inclusion and exclusion operations forming part of a classification grouping.[1] This is the significance of such implications from the viewpoint of elaborating a logic of meanings.

---

[1]By "grouping," Piaget refers to the structure of concrete operational thought, whose formal description shares some features (e.g., inverse operations) of algebraic groups (hence the label "grouping") as well as features (e.g., nested inclusions) of ordered sets or lattices. See Piaget, J., *Essai de Logique Opératoire*, Paris: Dunod, 1971; Wermus, H., "Formalisation de quelques structures initiales de la psychogenèse," *Archives de Psychologie*, 1973, *42*, 271-288; Wittmann, E., "Natural numbers and groupings," *Educational Studies in Mathematics*, 1975, *6*, 53-75. (P.M.D.)

Inhelder, B., & Piaget, J., *The Early Growth of Logic in the Child*, New York: Harper and Row, 1964, describes many such forms of classification. (J.E.)

The apparatus is a network of tunnels (dimensions: 110 x 50 cm; height: 5 cm; see Figure 2). The "tree" is positioned before the child with the trunk on the left and the branches expanding toward the right, in order to avoid artifacts that could arise from suggesting a "top" and a "bottom" of the tree. The trunk road T divides into two primary branches $A1$ and $A2$. Each of these in turn branches out in two paths $B1$ and $B2$ for $A1$, and $B3$ and $B4$ for $A2$. From each of these four Bs two further paths separate: $C1$ and $C2$ for $B1$; $C3$ and $C4$ for $B2$; $C5$ and $C6$ for $B3$; and $C7$ and $C8$ for $B4$. Each of the final paths ends up in one of eight garages G. The trunk T and all the ramifications are hollow tunnels, so that a small car entering T will necessarily end up in one of the eight Gs. The task is to determine what garage the car is in. For this purpose, the car is tied to a long thin ribbon, which lies between T and G after the car has arrived. Furthermore, each

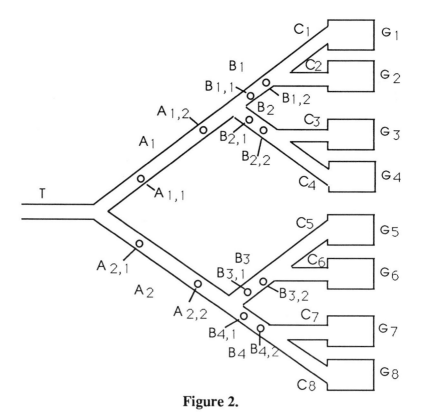

Figure 2.

A and *B* path is provided with two small round windows that the child may open (and must then reclose) to check if the ribbon is in the branch. The car can neither turn around nor go backwards.

One can see how many inferences and operations this experimental set up allows: If the ribbon is in *A*1, this implies that the car is located between *G*1 and *G*4, while *G*5 through *G*8 are excluded; if the ribbon is in *A*2, the car must have gone through *B*3 or *B*4; and so on. Because the classification grouping can take the form of a tree isomorphic to the present situation, we are shifting here from the study of sensorimotor implications to an analysis of implications among operations in a grouping. We assume these operations are based on meanings and are accompanied by verbal expressions of a nonextensional nature. We have been able to distinguish 4 levels: IA, IB, II and III.

1.   Level IA

Here are examples from level IA (about 4 to 5 years):

SAB (4;7) starts by opening all the *G*s until she finds the right one and, on request, she shows the route that has led to it. "Open only the windows that are useful in finding out." (She opens *A*1.)[2] "Yes—What does that mean?" *That the ribbon sticks to the car.* "Where will the car arrive?" *Here* (*G*1). *No* (the car is in *G*2). "In another?" *No*. "Just try." (*G*2: correct.) "Is it better to begin by opening windows in *A*, *B* or *C*?" *In* C. "Is it helpful to open any before that?" *No*. "In *B*" (for instance)? *No, that's useless.* "How about opening *C*?" *Yes.* "Why?" (No response.)

The car is put into *G*5. "Try to find out with a few windows only." (She opens *A*(1,1).) *No*. (She opens *A*(2,1).) *Yes*. She then opens *A*(2,2), which is useless because it's on the same segment, and then does likewise with *B*(4,1) and *B*(4,2): *No*. She nevertheless opens *G*7 and *G*8, which is inconsistent with the fact that *B*4 is empty. Then she opens *B*(3,1): *Yes*, but then opens *B*(3,2) (useless). "In what garage is the car?" She shows *G*4, *G*3, *G*2 and then *G*1, which branch out of *A*1 and are thus inconsistent with *A*2. Then she points to *G*5, by chance correct but also because it comes after *G*1-*G*4, which are wrong. "And when there is no ribbon?" *That doesn't mean anything.* "If the ribbon is in *B*1, where will the car be?" (She

---

[2]Specific windows are designated by ordered pairs, such that *A*(1,1) means the first window on branch *A*1, etc. Windows are also referred to more simply by the name of the branch (e.g., *A*1) when greater specificity is not needed.

shows $G1$-$G5$, whereas only $G1$-$G2$ are right.) Therefore, even though it is easy for *Sab* to go back from the *G*s to *T*, she can make no inclusion when going from *A* to *G*. "Is it useful to open windows in *A*?" *No*. "And in *B*?" *No, it's useless.*

XIS (4;11). "Is *A* useful?" *No, here* (*C*). How about there (*B*)?" *No*.

ERI (5;8). He opens the *G*s at random: "Would it be easier if we opened one of the *A*s first?" *No, because the car doesn't go up there.* "Would it work if we opened *A* or *B*?" *We might open the others, but it's better with the Cs because they are closer to garages.*

DAV (5;0) starts at *C* and opens seven *G*s before finding the right one (*G1*). When asked, he points out the route the car followed. Nonetheless, when the car is placed in *G6*, he points out successive *C*s. "Is that end there (*A*s) useful?" *No*. "Show me up further where the car has gone through." (He opens *B4*, whereas the arrival in *G6* implies *B3*.) "Has it gone through there?" *Yes, here* (he shows *A2* and *B4* [*G8*] and is surprised by the outcome, which he corrects by rightly opening *A2, B3*, and *G6*). "Try not to open a lot of doors: Is it good to open one in *A*?" *Yes* (he opens *A*(1,1) and *A*(1,2): useless; and goes on with *B*1). "Where can the car end up?" *There* (*G1*-*G4*, although *G3* and *G4* are excluded). "Couldn't the car get there (*G5*-*G8*)?" *No, because the ribbon isn't in* A2. For *G8*, however, he resumes focusing only on the *C*s.

If the elements *C*, *B* and *A* were objects which could be directly nested through inclusions, the problem would clearly be easier to solve. However, although the "grouping" involved here is isomorphic to a classification, in this infralogical or spatial version (where the *C*s emanate from a subdivision of the *B*s, and the *B*s similarly from the *A*s), the final positions result from the paths taken. This complicates things for the subjects, who are centered on the final positions without deducing the cars' paths from the starting point; consequently, even when the paths are comprehended they are devoid of necessity. Hence the paucity of implications, which only bear on the easy tracing of the path followed, once its end point *G* is known, and do not bear on predicting the path from *T* to *G*. As a matter of fact, such an anticipation is not based on simple implications of the form $A \rightarrow B$ (or $A1 \rightarrow B1$), but on an implication in which the antecedent term $A1$ entails a dichotomy $B1$ or $B2$ whose terms are reciprocally exclusive (notation w): $A1 \rightarrow (B1 \text{ w } B2)$, and so forth. Thus, what we meet here is a "grouping" of the normal form: $A + A' = B$, $B + B' = C$, ..., but which must be read and even constructed in the reverse order—$B \rightarrow (A \text{ w } A')$, $C \rightarrow (B \text{ w } B')$—instead of the direct order A, B, C, as is the case when the path is deduced from its end. As a result, in the opinion of most subjects, "it is useless" (*Sab*, *Xis* and *Dav*) to start from *T*, *A* or *B* because "the car doesn't go up there" (*Eri*). Thus, this first level is characterized by a lack of inclusions in the direction of the paths' construction, in spite of the ease with which the paths can be traced back.

2. Level IB

Between level I and the systematic inclusions starting at level IIA are a number of intermediate cases that display a mixture of correct implications of the form $A1 \rightarrow (B1 \vee B2)$ with inferences that are still invalid. In other words, there is a transition from a purely empirical method (the more or less exhaustive examination of the *G*s without taking the paths into account) to semi-empirical and semi-deductive procedures. More briefly, this level IB is characterized by partial inclusions.

HAD (5;6) starts with the *C*s, but on the second trial begins from $B1$ and $B3$ and, as they are empty, he opens $A2$, where he sees the ribbon. Skipping the *B*s, he deduces $C7$ and $C8$ and finds the car in $G8$. "Was it useful to open $B3$?" He answers *no*, in light of his success in going from $A2$ to $G8$ (the latter are on a straight line at the bottom of the apparatus). Asked to use just three windows, he chooses only $B2$ and $B3$, that is, one *B* on each primary branch.

RAC (6;6) starts with $B2$, then opens $B1$: *Ah, it's here*, then opens $G2$ (correct). On the second trial, she starts with $A2$, then opens $B4$ and $G8$, which is right again. On the third trial, however, from *non-A1*—she opens it twice, as if the second window $A(1,2)$ would correct the absence of the ribbon in $A(1,1)$—she directly concludes with $C4$ and $C5$, which are incompatible. Next from *non-A1* she directly infers $B2$, which does not derive from $A2$ but precisely from $A1$. "What does that mean, that the car isn't in $B1$?" *Ah! Now I understand everything; it will be in* $B2$ *because first it is in $A1$ and after, perhaps, it turns in* (i.e., *toward*) $B2$. However, from $B2$ she wrongly concludes $G8$, which depends upon $B4$; and so on. "Is it better to open a window in *A*?" *No, anywhere.* "Where is it better?" *In* A, B *and* C. She correctly adopts that order on the next trial, but then she resumes (as at level IA) enumerating the *C*s (to which she adds a *B*). So *Rac* strangely alternates correct deductions with periodic relapses into the false inferences of level IA.

GAB (6;0). Similarly, together with precise implications, *Gab* makes some that can be as wrong as these: $A1 \rightarrow B3 \rightarrow \{C4, C3, C2 \text{ and } C1\}$.

DAN (6;0) begins brilliantly with *A2, B3, C6. I found it!* "Could you have opened fewer windows?" *No.* He starts again, reaches *B3* and again shows *C6.* "Could it have been in another *G* (in fact *G5*)?" *No.* "Are you sure?" *Yes* (he opens *G5* and finds the car). "Does it help to start with *A*?" *Sometimes one may start with C because we always find it.* "And with *A*?" *Sometimes we find it; sometimes we don't find it.* "Is it better to start with *A* or with *C*?" *Sometimes it's better to start in the middle.*

LAU (6;1). He makes correct but easy inferences when he starts with *A, B, C,* and he gives the reason for the predicted arrival of the car in *G5* or *G6: Because it went through* B3 *and, as it cannot cross the roads from* B3 *to* B4, *it can only be in* C5 *and* C6. On the other hand, he sums up what he thinks by saying: *If we want to be sure where the car has gone through, we must start with* B, *because with* A *it can either go there* (top) *or there* (bottom). "So it's not necessary to open it at *A*?" *With* A *we can't tell later in what direction it goes; we must start with* B. "How about *C*?" *Yes, because we can see at once. The game is made in such a way that it is useless to start with* A *and* B. *Lau* completely disregards the "why" of the final positions, and thus disregards necessity.

MIC (6;2) goes even further: *To find the car, the* Cs *help a lot, the* Bs *help a little, and the* As *not at all.* This is the very negation of inclusions.

JAN (6;6), who is close to level IIA, starts with *A*, then *B* and *C*, and compares *A*1 with *A*2 or pairs of *B*s, and so forth: *Because you always put it on the other side; if the ribbon isn't there, we know that it is in the other one.* All this doesn't prevent him from eventually concluding that *to open the fewest windows we must start with the* Cs. He doesn't see that there are eight windows in that case and only three when one starts with *A*.

Thus, we notice that some of these reactions evidence partial inclusions, whereas others involve false inferences. As a result, all positions in *G* are finally discovered, but as static situations and not as the necessary outcome of the paths followed.

3. Levels II and III

It is only around age 7-8 years (level II) that the network is considered in its entirety and begins to constitute an operatory grouping. However, subjects at this level have not yet determined the necessary minimum number of windows that have to be opened, nor the possibility of succeeding by noticing positions where there is no ribbon, which stems from the fact that the system is dichotomous in each of its subdivisions. A few false inferences remain but they are soon corrected.

SEB (7;10). "To find it as soon as possible, shall we start in *A* or in *C*?" *In A.* He performs the right sequence *A*2, *B*3, *C*5. "Can we know how many windows we must open?" *No, it depends.*

BRI (8;6) correctly chooses *A*2, *B*4, *C*7. "Could you find out by opening fewer windows?" *I don't know.* Then he opens *A*2 (empty), *A*1, *B*2 (empty), *B*1, *G*2 (empty), *G*1 (right). "If you open *A*1 and you don't see the ribbon, is it useful?" *Yes, that means it has gone through the other one.*

DID (8;2) turns from *A*1 (empty) to *B*3. "In what *G* could it be?" *In G5.* "Could it be another?" *G*6. "In another one?" *No, because it has gone through B3 and because it cannot go back.* "With how many windows can we find out?" *Three.* "With less than that?" *Maybe.* "Are three windows always enough?" *More, sometimes.* "Is it possible to find out without seeing the ribbon?" *It isn't possible, for if there is no ribbon in A1, then it is in A2. If the ribbon isn't in B3, then it is in B4, and if not in C8, then in the other one* (C7). "So it is possible without seeing the ribbon?" *No, because I can't see where it is; we must see the ribbon.* "Can't we know in advance?" *No.* "If three windows aren't enough, how many more?" *Five.* "Show me again." *If not* B1, *then* B3. *If not* B3, *then* C7. "Will you be sure with 4 or 5 windows?" *Yes.*

At a slightly more advanced level, the subjects assert that it is necessary always to start with *A* and that opening three windows suffices to find the car:

YVA (8;11) opens *A*2, *B*4 (failure), then *B*3, *G*6: *No. Then it is in G5 because I saw the ribbon in A2 and not here* (B4, etc.); *so the car cannot be in G7 and G8. Now, I opened one door too many because if the ribbon wasn't in B4, it went through B3.* "Is it possible to succeed with fewer doors?" *Yes, one less.* "Even less?" *No, I must see if (it is in)* A1 *or* A2.

SAD (8;3): *It's in G3 because it has gone through A1 and B2 and not through C4.* "Must we start with *A*?" *Yes, always, because when we open A, we already know on what side the ribbon is.* "And if we can't see the ribbon anywhere?" *That sort of helps; if we see it, that helps too.* "Can we find it, if we never see it, beginning with *A*?" *No, impossible. We have to see it at least once or twice.*

Thus, these subjects have attained a nearly complete necessity, which nevertheless lacks the form of necessity that characterizes level III — the possibility of specifying the necessary path by opening only empty windows:

VER (9;9) begins with level II reactions, which is normal at her age, but she always follows the order *A, B, C.* However, after being asked, "Could the car have taken another path to arrive there?", she only has level III reactions: *No, the car was compelled.* "With how many windows can we know?" *With three.* "Why?" *Because this* (A2) *is a path, these two* (B3 or B4) *make up another path and this* (a C) *is another one.* "Is it compulsory to open three of them?" *Yes, three is compulsory.* "Is the order important?" (She shows the *A*s.) *We are obliged to start with* A. "Now what happens when there is no ribbon?" *That means the car has gone through the other one.*

CAT (10;3): *If we open* A1 *and don't see anything, the car has gone through* A2. *If we open* B3 *and don't see anything, then it has gone through* B4; *and if there is nothing in* G7, *then it has gone to* G8. *Three windows are always enough.* "Does it help if we see something?" *Yes.* "And if we don't see anything?" *Yes.*

CRI (11;1). "Does it help to see the ribbon?" *Yes.* "What if we don't see it?" *Yes. That means that if it's not on this side it's on the other side.* "Does that help as much?" *Yes.*

STE (11;8). About seeing nothing: *If we skip a hole here* (at B), *that doesn't help. If we do it in the right order, that helps.* "Is it possible to find the garage without ever seeing the ribbon?" *Yes.* "Isn't this strange?" *No, one must* (i.e., *one only needs to*) *be logical.* "Are you quite sure?" *Yes.*

DAC (12;11) states that three windows are necessary, *because there are three segments.* And, *it's always kind of an opposite* (i.e., dichotomy). "If we don't see the ribbon?" *It is as if we had left a clear trace.*

PHA (12;2). "If we never see the ribbon?" *Yes, we can find out by opening three windows.*

This negative necessity, as it were, is thus the most difficult aspect for the subjects to accept. However, it is the criterion of understanding the whole system as a set of dichotomies that explain the arrival points in *C* and *G*, without depending on empirical (or half-empirical, half-inferential) verifications. This system is a grouping, although a spatial (infralogical) one which doesn't pertain to classifying discrete objects but rather to chaining paths. As such, it brings up a problem: Operational classifications are constructed around age 7 or 8, with the understanding of inclusions and their quantifications (i.e., if $B = A + A'$, then $B > A$ and $B > A'$), whereas in the present case the grouping is operationally complete only around age ten or twelve.

The reason for this situation is clear, and instructive as well: the successful classifications at age 7 or 8 are constructed in an ascending order, from the particular to the more and more general (i.e., in the form $A + A' = B, B + B' = C, C + C' = D$, etc; where the notation "+" designates constrained conjunction).[3] By contrast, in the present situation, the required operations consist of reconstructions in a descending order: $D = C$ or C'; $C = B$ or B'; $B = A$ or A'. These reconstructions replace the conjunctions "+" ("and") with successive disjunctions ("or"). The reason for this substantial décalage between the "or" and the "and" is seemingly that when constructing a grouping, one is restricted to adding new elements, whether in the already constituted classes, or in a more general class that includes them; in the descending method involving a series of disjunctions, one must always reason about "possibilities" while considering each tier of the system.

4.   Conjunctions, disjunctions and binary operations

Well before they understand the whole system of the paths followed, the subjects clearly are able to perform some local disjunctions, that is, to use "or" in various particular situations. Similarly, the experiment in chapter 1 shows that children who have taken the dog out of its box can move it either to the right or to the left before pulling it back. These contingent and limited combinations between "and" and "or"[4] may therefore take forms that are isomorphic to the 16 binary operations of a systematic propositional logic. But in the present case, they are nothing

---

[3]*Constrained conjunction* denotes one of the "peculiarities" of groupings: "The compositions of a grouping apply only *contiguously*; that is, they are relative to the dichotomous complementarities from which the grouping is structured" (*Essai de Logique*, p. 107). In other words, grouping operations are defined in terms of relevance and shared meanings: "The grouping is an intensive, not an extensive, construct, but one that is well defined..." (*Essai de Logique*, p. 93). This property of groupings, little loved by logicians, underscores the continuity between Piaget's earlier formalizations of natural logic and the present treatment. (P.M.D.)

[4]Including, of course, exclusions or negations.

more than temporary coordinations of actions, which simultaneously generate the "and" and "or," with the possibility of exclusions as likely as that of positive implications. Such localized, precocious coordinations are of course expanded when "groupings" are achieved. In that case, according to the direction of inference, $B = A + A'$ yields the implication: If x is a B, it is necessarily "either" an A, "or" an A'.

Let us now give a few examples:

• To begin with, our paths are obviously based on implications of the form $B1 \rightarrow A1$, where the arrow $\rightarrow$ (implication symbol) expresses the fact that going through $A1$ is a preliminary condition for continuing to $B1$, whereas the reciprocal implication $A1 \leftarrow B1$ states that going through $B1$ is one of the consequences of going through $A1$.

• On the other hand, there is no implication in the relations such as that between $B1$ and $C5$ (i.e., we have either $p \cdot \overline{q}$, and thus $\overline{p \rightarrow q}$; or $\overline{p} \cdot q$, and thus $\overline{q \rightarrow p}$).

• The most frequent binary connectives are the conjunction "and" in an ascending order and the exclusive disjunction "or" (p w q) in a descending order.

• Non-exclusive disjunctions $(p \cdot \overline{q})\vee(\overline{p} \cdot q)\vee(p \cdot q)$ may be observed, for instance, when the subject has seriated 3 elements $A < B < C$ (these triplets can appear very early) and sees that if A is the only one smaller than the others and C bigger, the "medium" element B is both $<$ and $>$.

• We notice incompatibility $(p \cdot \overline{q})\vee(\overline{p} \cdot q)\vee(\overline{p} \cdot \overline{q})$ between, for example, the pairs $(G5, G6)$ and $(G7, G8)$, which can be written $(p \cdot \overline{q})\vee(\overline{p} \cdot q)$. In this case, $G1$ through $G4$ would be neither p nor q $(= \overline{p} \cdot \overline{q})$.

• Conjunct negation may therefore appear quite early: In the case of the tools in chapter I, when the subject understands how to draw back the animal, he excludes the two actions of pushing and lateral shifting, thus $\overline{p} \cdot \overline{q}$.

• Equivalence $(p \cdot q)$w$(\overline{p} \cdot \overline{q})$ is evident when the subject understands that the dichotomy ("you always put it on the other side", says Jan at age 6) is repeated in all subdivisions.

• We may speak of "tautology" when it is obvious for the child (who doesn't need to express it) that the ribbon must be in exactly one of the branches at a given rank, and in none of the others.

• By contrast, the connective "contradiction" or "always false," consists only of specific contradictions to be avoided, which the subject doesn't always do (for instance, in preinstrumental behavior, the younger subjects merely perform erroneous displacements without even pulling the object).

• As for the "affirmations" or "negations" involved in the independence of p with respect to q [$(p \cdot q) \vee (p \cdot \bar{q})$], or of q with respect to p, these are obvious at all ages and there is no need to deal with them here.

Our first conclusion is that some partial and sometimes only temporary coordinations are present at elementary levels, in forms which may be compared with the 16 binary operations of classical logic. These coordinations do not depend on the structured wholes which become possible only at the level of true formal operations, characterized by hypothetical-deductive thinking and the INRC group. From the standpoint of a logic of meanings, this fact is of importance in demonstrating that from the beginning, "forms" partially depend upon contents while remaining necessary for assimilating them.

The second lesson we draw from this research is that one of the major and even constitutive conditions of formal thought (at level III) is the late acquisition of systematic and permanent coordinations between "and" and "or," with respect to distinct ascending and descending methods of going through a given system.

3

TILING

With B. Vitale and M. Zinder

We shall now go back to action implications, with a study whose interest is twofold as it bears both on a practical problem and on combinations of geometrical shapes. The practical problem is to lay the floor with tiles so that no empty space will be left between the tiles and so the pattern could be continued indefinitely. The tiles have various geometrical shapes (Figure 3): squares S (yellow), isosceles triangles T (white), pentagons P (blue) and hexagons H (red). The sides of S, P and H and the base of T have the same length (8 cm), and the angles of T are such that when placed next to P their sides make a straight extension of P. All figures are available to the subjects, who may lay them out either by using identically shaped elements (a tessellation composed only of squares is the easiest to construct without gaps, whereas this is impossible using only pentagons) or by mixing shapes in various ways (for instance, when filling the gaps in an arrangement of pentagons with triangles).

We may analyze two kinds of action implications. First, some implications only anticipate arrangements that can be made with similar figures: for instance, predicting that juxtapositions of squares will tile the floor without gaps, and above all (and this is a separate issue), that if such a tiling is possible on a small surface, it can be continued indefinitely. Conversely, a juxtaposition of pentagons will leave "holes" that cannot be corrected by adding more pentagons.

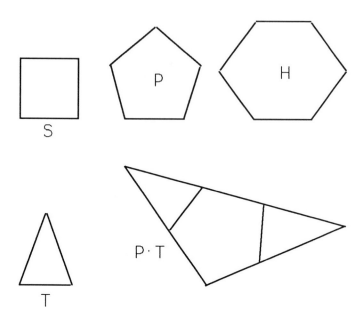

Figure 3.

Second, there are other forms of inferences that are actually more interesting. If one can make a complete tiling with squares, without any triangle (in our notation, $S \cdot \bar{T}$) or with triangles without any square (in our notation, $T \cdot \bar{S}$), is it possible to combine the two? For example:

$(T \cdot \bar{S}) \vee (S \cdot \bar{T}) \rightarrow (T \cdot S) = Sc$ (success);

$(T \cdot \bar{P}) \vee (P \cdot \bar{T}) \rightarrow (T \cdot P) = Sc$;

whereas $(S \cdot \bar{P}) \vee (P \cdot \bar{S}) \rightarrow (S \cdot P) = \bar{Sc}$ (failure).

These inferences raise several questions: whether subjects who succeed in constructing a tiling with Ts only or Ss only will conclude that a gapless tiling can be formed by combining Ts and Ss; whether a successful combination $T \cdot P$ demonstrates that the tiling is possible with Ps only, which is wrong, or with Ts only, which is easy; and whether the fact that $T \cdot P$ is possible entails $S \cdot P$, actually an impossible combination. In all these cases, the inferences pertain to relations between heterogenous and homogeneous patterns, which supposes much more advanced and complex anticipations.

Moreover, in this study, we shall meet again the 16 binary operations we dealt with in chapter 2. There are three clearly distinct levels of performance.

1. Level I

Subjects at this first stage only succeed in setting out a gapless tiling with squares, and without inferring that the tiling could go on indefinitely; thus they fail even this elementary form of recurrential reasoning.

NAD (6;7) assembles six squares in a rectangle: *Like this, we can do it.* "Can you always add some without leaving holes?" *No, I don't think so* (she adds some on the longer side of the figure). "Well, you can continue, can't you?" *Yes* (she has now laid down 12 squares). *We can go on like this, make an even bigger one.* "As big as you wish?" *No.* "If you put two of them this way (two squares, making a rectangle), what do you call them?" *I call them a triangle because they have a height.* "How can you know that a figure is a square?" *Because it has the shape of a square.* "How about that one (a 5x6 cm rectangle she has constructed)?" *Not entirely* (a square). With hexagons and three squares, she composes a long snake and then flowers with triangular gaps between their petals. She points to a gap and says, *afterwards I want to do* (i.e., *to lay down) something there.* "Will you be able to fill all these holes" (there are only four of them)? *No, I think we shall never be able to do it; there will always be holes.*

DAN (6;8) starts with a nice crown composed of 10 pentagons which are joined side by side, leaving a large hole in the middle of the figure. He tries to fill it with three elements: *No, we cannot fill it because there and there* (he shows the remaining gaps) *they don't have the same shape as this one!* Then he lays out 17 pentagons in two parallel rows, separated by a space where he puts nine more *P*s. *We cannot do it.* He refuses to use other shapes (*H*s). Nevertheless, he later sets out a new tiling with *H*s only and he notes that this works *because they all have the same shape.* This is in contradiction with what he accepted for *P*s. "And with both" (*P*s and *H*s together)? *With H*s, *yes, but with P*s, *no.* He constructs rosettes with an *H* surrounded by *P*s and draws the conclusion that *we cannot cover.* "Why?" *Because there* (H) *it isn't square.*

COR (7;9) is nearing level II but she cannot really overcome level I difficulties. She starts with *S*s, setting out a rectangular mosaic of 18 pieces. "Could we continue?" *Yes, perhaps, and sometimes no.* "Why?" She adds a vertical and then a horizontal appendage to the rectangle, both composed of three elements. Then she couples them with the initial figure, but with a displacement such that one side of the adjoined squares corresponds to two half-sides of the central square. Like *Dan*, she reacts by using *H*s, then merely produces very irregular alignments or surfaces with a mixture of *S*s and *H*s.

These initial reactions are first of all remarkable for the lack of any anticipation they display throughout the questioning, to such a point that one might suppose these subjects do not understand the instruction to fill all gaps. But this is not the case. Most curious is the example of the squares, since at age 6, the child obviously understands it is possible to prolong any linear series ($n \rightarrow n+1$). Yet, *Nad* and even *Cor* seem blocked at the idea of indefinitely widening a surface, even one as simple and gapless as a set of squares juxtaposed in a regular way along two dimensions. On the other hand, although she plans to "put something there" to fill four small triangular holes, *Nad* peremptorily concludes that "we shall never be able to do it; there will always be holes." Another strange reaction is to start with a long snake while not forgetting that the goal is to set out a tiling. In sum, the characteristic of level I is the empiricism with which the subjects are satisfied, along with minimal inferences, most of which are not justified—such as *Dan*'s idea that surrounding an *H* with *S*s would better cover the whole surface than surrounding it with *P*s.

2. Level II

At 7-8 years, we notice some progress in inferences and in certain combinations of variously shaped elements:

PAU (6;9) starts with a flower: an *H* surrounded by *T*s standing on their bases. To find out if she can continue, however, she removes the *T*s. "Can we go on like this?" *I don't know but I'm sure* (!). She lays down about 50 of them. *Now we're sure we can go on.* Then she places about 24 *T*s in an irregular figure but without gaps, before better arranging the whole. With *P*s, she constructs a large crown and, to fill its empty interior space, she replaces *H*s by *T*s, which she places in a circle with apexes in the center.

XAV (7;5) starts with *T*s only, arranged in an irregular global shape, and fills the gaps with other *T*s without regard for the shape as a whole. He concludes, *I could always continue like this. I think there will be no holes because it's tight.* "Could we cover the whole room?" *Yes, its possible to do this in the whole room.* He chooses another global shape and builds a fine rosette with eight *T*s, apexes touching at the center, but then he becomes critical: "Shall we always be able to fill the holes?" *That won't fill when it's round at the edges* (that is, when the figure is inserted in a square space like the room). *We could make a larger square* (he assembles 15 *S*s to form a large rectangle and asserts it is possible to go on doing the same). "And with the *S*s and the *T*s?" *No, we can't.* But he actually does so by juxtaposing two squares of four at one of their corners, filling the intervals with *T*s.

BEA (7;10). While arranging *P*s in a crown, she can't fill the gaps, whereas with four *H*s she immediately sees that *we can go on and on.* After succeeding with *S*s and *T*s, she concludes: *With Ts only I can make it, with Ss only I can make it, but not with Ss and Ts* (together).[1] She spontaneously tries with *P*s and *S*s; making a crown of *P*s, with an *S* and a few *T*s in the middle. This fails, but she succeeds with an *H* and *T*s: *I could always go on like this.*

AUG (8;10). First, he makes a crown with *P*s without knowing how to fill up the center. Nevertheless, he becomes the first child to join four *P*s side to side with corners pointed up, capped by another row of *P*s with corners pointed down, the intervals then filled in with *T*s: *And then we can go on.* When gathering three *H*s in an arc of a circle, he notices that the inner gap itself is shaped like an *H*: *We could go on a lot; that's because of the shape* (he shows the empty space). When continuing with *T*s and *H*s, he says: *I didn't know if this would work; perhaps it will.* "We know that we can make it with the *T*s and also with the *H*s; isn't it natural that we should succeed with both?" *No, we can't be sure; we must try.*

PAC (8;9) composes seven *H*s with *S*s on the external sides. "Can we fill it up?" *No, each time we add an S, it will make a new hole.*

BEN (9;10) gathers three closely joined *H*s in a triangular shape and, like *Aug*, he says, *We can always put more there because the hole has the same shape* (i.e., *H*).

---

[1]The operation can be symbolized (where Sc = Success):

$$[(S \rightarrow Sc) \cdot (T \rightarrow Sc)] \rightarrow Sc; \text{ or } [(S \rightarrow Sc) \cdot (T \rightarrow Sc)] \rightarrow (S \cdot T \rightarrow Sc).$$

The same operations are seen with *Xav*.

JOS (9;8). She assembles four *P*s and four *T*s: *Here we may go on with T*s. Her overall conclusion: *With T*s *only we can succeed (Sc), with P*s *only we cannot (Sc* = true), *with both P*s *and T*s *we cannot (Sc* = false), *with T*s *and H*s *we cannot (Sc* = false), *and with P*s *and H*s *we cannot either (Sc* = true).

Such reactions are interesting in that inferences are developed in the form of action implications, either for anticipating the figures to be made or for deducing a possible continuation. As to the first point, total anticipations are rare; instead, the subjects consider the remaining gaps and predict how they are going to fill them. On the other hand, regarding the second point, a very general implication is that any gapless figure implies its possible continuation (with the exception of circular figures, which must remain circular, e.g., *Xav*). When it comes to the reasons for such a continuation, *Pau* "doesn't know but is sure." By contrast, *Aug* and *Ben* construct figures with *H*s only and discover a reason in the shape of the gaps, which are also *H*s. Conversely, the subjects see perfectly well that *P*s surrounded by *S*s will never cover the whole surface since "each time we add an *S*, it will make a new hole" (*Pac*). However, despite these various advances, the deductions characterizing this level are still inadequate, especially when the children must predict combinations of two differently shaped tiles (for example, *Jos*'s difficulty even at age 9).

3.   Level III

It is at this last level that inferences and action implications play a critical role, both through their rigor and their productivity:

MAC (11;4) builds two rosettes with concentric *T*s, but fills the intervals with other *T*s. "Can we go on" (without creating holes)? *We can go on to have an indefinite surface because it always looks the same and I can imagine this surface is very large: We can demonstrate that, this way, it will become infinite.* "Why?" *Because it fills everything; therefore, if we continued, it would be the same.* He makes a new surface, this time symmetrically. "Why?" *All shapes with a straight side can be folded in two parts, which makes symmetry axes. I think we can make them.* The experimenter draws a figure with an aberrant circumference: *I think we can make it.*

CAR (11;4) has the same initial reactions as *Mac*. Then with *P*s she predicts at once that one can fill the holes with *T*s, and therefore with *P*s only *there will always be a hole.* She complements two adjoined *P*s with four *T*s and declares:

That's it, I made a parallelogram and we've seen that in that case we can go on.
"Did you know beforehand that there was a solution (using *T, S, P,* which she has just done) or did you discover that?" *We could know* (she points at the separate parts).

ARC (11;6). After mixing *P*s and *T*s, he says: *The figure would be irregular, but perhaps it's possible to go on like this* (without gaps). "And if we add *S*s?" *I think it's possible—I am even sure.* Nevertheless, he keeps to a regular shape and he feels confident when he obtains a parallelogram: *I know we can make an infinite surface with a parallelogram; the same with S s only, and also with Hs.* If all shapes were mixed: *That would be a bit difficult but it's possible if we measure the angles* (which are, with respect to the gaps, obtuse or acute). *We can't make something with Ps only.*

ANI (12;2) also starts with *P*s and *T*s but, although she asserts that a continuation is possible, she says: *That's annoying because there is always something to put* (i.e., *to add in the gaps*), *but it's always rather in a mess: We can't prove anything.* Then as *Arc* did, she tries to form regular wholes. While acknowledging that one *can always go on with mixed shapes,* she is very please to obtain: *A parallelogram! At last, this makes a surface* (a regular one)! *We see that we can add to infinity, but here I don't know* (how to prove it). *That's annoying: I can always add something but, well, I'm bothered: It's not a regular law, we add randomly.*

These higher level subjects are interesting for the requirements they set. Of course they accept that once a limited gapless surface is found, even if by partial anticipations and step-by-step observations, it will always be possible to reproduce it indefinitely by complementing the figure at its connecting sides. It is possible as well to merely widen the initial surface indefinitely: *Mac* calls it a "demonstration that it will become infinite this way." He is slightly more satisfied when he endows his figures with symmetry axes; this marks a beginning regularity which warrants iterations through resemblances. With *Car,* the need for regularity becomes clear: Obtaining "parallelograms" not only insures but demonstrates the possible continuation—which is a much stronger requirement than before; moreover, the variations in the shapes of gaps may be compensated through complementary variations in the angles. Finally, with *Arc* and *Ani,* there is sharp difference between regular shapes, on the one hand, from which "infinite surfaces" can be necessarily deduced, and irregular shapes on the other hand, which undoubtedly can be continued through variable adjustments, but which pose an "annoying mess" (*Ani*) instead of a simple demonstration.

4. Conclusions

This study is of special value in clarifying the evolution of the three types of inferences which characterize our three levels. At level I, the anticipations are limited to those allowed by observable repeated arrangements, or through empirically observed modifications. At level II, the inferences relate to predictions that go beyond the observable and are based on necessary implications, but without providing "reasons." Finally, at level III, the inferences are based on reasons or on possible demonstrations.

i. At level I action implications come down to the two following types: (1) A gap in the tiling can (or must) be filled by a similarly shaped element (S, H, etc.); and (2), once a configuration is completed in a limited space, it can be widened: "We can go on like this, make an even bigger one" (*Nad*), or "yes, perhaps, and sometimes no" (*Cor*). On the other hand, it is not possible to make it "as big as you wish." *Nad* resolutely answers "no", as if "going on like this" presented limits and "making it even bigger" did not entail an indefinite iteration analogous to the succession of natural numbers: $n \rightarrow (n + 1)$. The reason for such a limitation is obviously that the recurrence (the "always") is not observable and the subject still reasons or infers only with respect to a domain of empirical objects. We have already seen elsewhere[2] that, when asked to put n, $n + 1$, etc., objects in a transparent container with one hand, while doing the same in a screened container with the other hand, subjects at this level affirm the equality of the two quantities, but aren't at all sure that this would still be the case if they went on adding objects "till the evening comes."

At level II, this unlimited continuation is inferred not only as being possible, but necessary, although without demonstration. When *Pau* asserts "I don't know but I'm sure," she likely means "I can neither demonstrate nor justify this, but being able to continue step by step necessarily implies that such a continuation is unlimited." This affirma-

[2]Piaget, J., & Inhelder, B. *The Child's Construction of Quantities: Conservations and Atomism.* New York: Basic Books, 1974.

tion reminds us of a young subject we often quote: "When we know once, we know forever." In other words, the action implication here is based on a reflective abstraction and isn't restricted, as at level I, to drawing logical consequences from empirical abstractions as in the inference, "If I have succeeded in making this assemblage without creating any gap, then I can widen it."

Finally, at level III, subjects distinguish what *Ani* calls "an annoying mess" which she is sure she can prolong indefinitely without deducing the detailed operations (because "we add at random"), from what she calls a "surface" (i.e., a regular and simple configuration). As a matter of fact, she discovers that she may construct "a parallelogram: At last this makes a surface!" She means that an iteration may be demonstrated through a set of easily deducible connections. This search for regularities appears first with *Mac*, who acts so certain about finding symmetry axes, even in an aberrant shape he is presented with, and is manifested further by *Car* and *Arc* who, like *Ani*, construct parallelograms. *Arc* says, "I know that with a parallelogram we can make an infinite surface."

Thus, we may distinguish three forms of action implications. The first one may be called a "conditioning" implication because it pertains to the necessary and sufficient conditions of success; in this case, finding elements which have the same shape as the gap. Such implications, which may be observed as early as level I, enable subjects to be sure they can "widen" or repeat what they have just made, but do not permit an infinite generalization, for one never knows what can happen.

We may call the second form an "amplifying" implication in that it bears on the consequences of what has already been begun. This is what happens at level II, and it may be explained as follows: If one succeeds in widening what is already made, then there is no reason one couldn't continue (see *Xav*'s responses).

The third form, which may be called a "justifying" implication, gives the reasons which allow an indefinite reiteration. In the case of regularly shaped configurations, such reasons are obtained through an easy demonstration (*Ani*'s "surfaces," which she contrasts with the initial "mess").

ii. Beyond these kinds of implications, considering that all three are valid in principle, we may add what we call *assumed* or *weak* implications. These are based on partial information, and yet they seem to be logically defensible. A typical occurrence is when the subject knows what can be made with *x* shapes exclusively and also with *y* shapes exclusively, and is asked to predict $x \cdot y$; that is, to predict what both x and y, with no additional support from a third form z, will produce. For instance, let us assume that Ss produce a gapless surface and that Ps produce a surface containing gaps. It is rather logical to predict that $S \cdot P$ will also have gaps. In the paradoxical case when exclusive Ss and exclusive Hs are both successful (Sc), the subject is induced to believe that $S \cdot H$ should succeed at least as well—whereas, in fact, they produce triangular gaps, and success becomes possible only with the ternary association $S \cdot H \cdot T$. In this case, despite its seemingly logical form, the implication $S \cdot H \rightarrow Sc$ can be maintained only as long as additional information through observations and anticipations has not been obtained.

These "assumed implications" vary in our three levels. At level I, children tend to lay out only homogeneous tilings without coordinating shapes, so the problem doesn't arise. When it is raised by the experimenter, the subject will answer like Dan who, when asked about Ps and Hs together, only affirms that the tiling is possible with each of them taken separately.

At level II, one finds a mixture of right answers, wrong answers and refusals to draw conclusions. For instance, Bea (7;10) asserts that there is success (Sc) with Ts alone and Ss alone, but she predicts failure ($\overline{Sc}$) with both Ss and Ts, which is wrong. Aug (8;10) is wrong or refuses to make any judgment: Ts only or Ss only are successful, but a combination of Ts and Ss is not. When asked about both Ts and Hs, he answers: *I didn't know if this would work. Perhaps it will.* "We know that we can make it with the Ts and also with the Hs; isn't it natural that we should succeed with both?" *No, we can't be sure, we must try it out.* As for Jos (9;8), she gives a series of right and wrong answers: One will succeed with Ts only, but not with Ps only, nor with both Ps and Ts ($\overline{Sc}$ = wrong), nor with both Ts and Hs ($\overline{Sc}$ = wrong), and "with Ps and Hs we can't either" ($\overline{Sc}$ = correct).

It is only at level III that the problem is solved. Car is even able to achieve a ternary composition $T \cdot S \cdot P$, asserting that it is deductively predictable and showing the detailed composition supporting this deduction. As for the question of assumed or non-validated implications, level III is interesting in that the subjects tend to focus at once—and often constantly—on the relations between two, three or four figures rather than on isolated shapes considered as absolutes. This relativization of course plays an important role in the search for demonstrations or "reasons."

iii. We still have to deal with operations on interrelated meanings, which, as we have said, are isomorphic with respect to the 16 interpropositional connectives. Let us first notice that there is no difference here between the meanings of objects and the meanings of actions. As the goal set for the subject is to achieve a gapless mosaic, the meaning of actions consists of success or failure and is thus based on the outcomes of manipulations. The meanings of objects amount to "what can be done with them," thus referring in all cases to actions performed on them. In the abstract, the objects may be classified with respect to their shape, as *Nad* initially does at level IA, or they may be seriated with respect to the number of sides they have (from 3 for *T*s to 6 for *H*s), and such a seriation is implicit at all levels. However, in the task context, the meaning of objects lies in the possibility or impossibility of achieving the required tiling. In this situation, the links the subject establishes or tries to establish turn out to be isomorphic with the familiar 16 interpropositional operations. This is not surprising since the task involves an elementary combinatorial system and since the only truth values in the subjects' statements just describe what they have been doing and the reasons for their success or failure.

To begin with, we may distinguish the four operations expressing the independence of *p*, *q*, or their negations, which are usually written as follows:

$$(p \cdot q) \vee (p \cdot \overline{q}), (\overline{p} \cdot q) \vee (\overline{p} \cdot \overline{q}), (p \cdot q) \vee (\overline{p} \cdot q) \text{ and } (\overline{p} \cdot \overline{q}) \vee (p \cdot \overline{q}).$$

These occur when the subject tries to construct a tiling with one of the four shapes without relating them to others, which is successful with *T*, *S* and *H* but fails with *P*.

Second, there are the conjunctions $(p \cdot q)$, which from the standpoint of meanings have two distinct forms: "Free" conjunctions such as $T \cdot S$, which are successful when the two shapes are combined as well as when they are separate; and "constrained" conjunctions such as $P \cdot T$. About the latter, a level III subject says that one succeeds by using *P*s because "we have added *T*s anyhow."

Third, we find the equivalent of exclusive disjunctions or reciprocal exclusions in the case of $H \cdot S$, a combination which, without a third shape, always fails. Nonexclusive disjunction is illustrated by the case $(T \cdot \overline{S}) \vee (\overline{T} \cdot S) \vee (T \cdot S)$ [compare $(p \cdot q) \vee (p \cdot \overline{q}) \vee (\overline{p} \cdot q)$].

Finally, we can clearly observe equivalences, as well as combinations that correspond to ternary operations. In all cases, only actions and their meanings are involved. Extensional propositions are not, even if subjects translate what they do into accurate verbal statements.

4

ARITHMETICAL IMPLICATIONS AND MEANINGS

With I. Berthoud and H. Kilcher

We have seen in chapters 1 to 3 that action implications play an essential role with respect to external objects and in problems that require reaching a goal and thus involve only practical successes and failures. What happens when the relevant objects are entities created by the subject, such as numbers, and when the permissible answers can only be translated in terms of "right" or "wrong"—that is, truth values? Shall we have to admit that the only implications involved are implications among statements? Or will we find that statements only verbally describe or formulate a set of operations, the implications being the actual and necessary origin of what statements convey at the level of communication?

This chapter accordingly tackles a problem that is not only essential for us but also has a general epistemological significance. Since we must distinguish between "intuitive" mathematics at the level of invention and "axiomatic" mathematics at the level of the most compelling demonstrations, it is natural to investigate the role played by implications between operations at the first level and what remains of them at the second. Similarly, if we do not interpret the term "constructivism" according to Brouwer's restricted meaning, then intuitive mathematics obviously consists of continuous constructions of operations whose meanings are interrelated by innumerable implications. In the following pages, we shall analyze the genesis of such coordinations as they take place in elementary situations.

The chapter is divided into two sections. The first deals with the relations between ordinal and cardinal numbers and with their mutual implications. The second section is an analysis of some of the preliminary and necessary conditions of counting, specifically counting in a circular order.

SECTION I: ORDINAL AND CARDINAL NUMBERS

The first experimental apparatus simply consists of two boxes (Figure 4). Connecting the higher one (H) and the lower one (L) is an opaque pipe through which marbles can be dropped one at a time by hand. The ordinal aspect of the task arises from the ordering of elements going from H to L as a function of the temporal succession of drops, whereas the cardinal aspect arises from the number of elements remaining in H or collected in L after each drop; that is, it refers to the states of H and L (before a drop is performed, when the nth marble is dropped, when it has arrived in L, etc.). The cardinal numbers in H and L are obviously complementary with respect to the total amount of marbles: $T = H + L$. Questions may address anticipations (before dropping the marbles) or reconstitutions (after the drops), the contents of the boxes naturally being hidden from view.

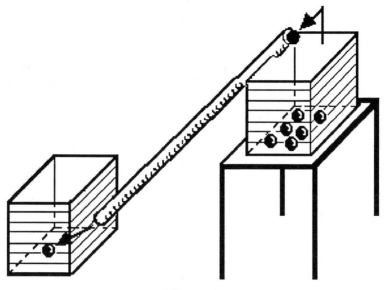

Figure 4.

We devised two experimental situations. In situation I, the total T initially amounts to 11 marbles in H (or less than 11 for younger subjects) and 0 in L. The children first are asked to predict: "Before the 5th marble drops, how many marbles will there be in L, and in H?" They are then asked to perform the action: "Let the marbles drop one at a time and stop before the 5th drops." H and L are then covered and the same questions about their cardinal numbers are asked. Thus, in this situation, the child must infer cardinal numbers from ordinal information.

In situation II, the sum T is 15 marbles in H. The subjects are asked to predict: "You are going to let 10 marbles drop from H into L, one at a time. Will the 4th be in L or in H? And the 7th? The 10th? Which marbles will be in H? The 13th? Which other marbles?" Then they are told, "Let 10 marbles drop into L." Once the action is performed, H and L are covered and the questions are repeated about which ordinals will be found in each box. Here, ordinals must be inferred from information about cardinals and the implications involved are reciprocal to those required in situation I.

We have been able to establish four levels.

1. Level IA

To begin with, here are examples from the first level, characterized by difficulty in dissociating the whole T into complementary subsets L and H, at least (or primarily) in situation I:

BRI (5;0). Situation I, action phase, with $T = 8$. "Stop before the 4th drops." (She drops 5.) "How many are there in L?" (No response.) "You did this five times with your hand. So, how many are there in L?" *Five.* "And in H?" *I don't know.* The child is given eight marbles again. "Stop after the 4th....How many of them have you already dropped?": *Three.*[1] "How many are left in H?" *Seven.* Again, with $T = 4$: "Stop before the 3rd falls." *Three of them will be in* L. "And in H, then?" *Four.* Situation II, with $T = 7$: "I've put 5 down there—Where is the 2nd?" (No response.)

---

[1] A 6-year-old girl once explained to me the spatial meaning of "before" and "after" in her statement, "3 comes after 4 and 5 comes before 4." She said that the numbers are arranged in order, starting with one, and as you move along them, you notice which number is still ahead (before) and which one is just behind you (after). Such an image might explain *Bri*'s failure to understand the interviewer's temporal meanings of these two words. (J.E.)

DAN (5;6). Situation I, anticipation phase: "How many marbles will be in *L* before the 5th drops?" *I think there won't be any.* "Will there be some, or not?" *Yes, 11.* So it is everything or nothing. Five marbles are then dropped: "How many are there in *L*?" *Five.* "What do you call the one that is about to fall?" *The six.* "How many are still in *H*?" *Six, no 11.* "Why did you say 6?" *I think my counting was wrong.*

Situation II with *T* = 10, 5 of which are dropped: "Is the 3rd in *L* or in *H*?" *In L.* "Why?" *Because it was put in the pipe.* "Where is the 5th?" *In L.* "And the 7th?" *In H.* "Which other one is in *H*?" *The 8.*

Situation I is repeated with 8 marbles in *H*: "We stop before throwing the 4th. Where is the 4th?" *In H.* "How many are there in *L*?" *There aren't any.* "Why?" *Because it's all empty.* "And how many in *H*?" *I don't know.* "Could you tell?" *About 8, but no, about 6, no 10, I think.*

CAT (5;6). Situation I, action phase, with *T* = 10: "Let 7 marbles drop into *L*" (She drops all 10). *There will be 7 because there were 10.* "But I asked you to drop only 7." *We can never have 7 with 10.* So the total cardinal *T* is not dissociated. As for actions, to "stop before the 5th" she counts *one* for the action of taking the 1st, *two* when she throws it in the pipe, *three* for the 2nd, *four* for the 3rd, and she concludes: *I let drop 4.* "At the beginning, we had 11 in *H*. You dropped 4 in *L*. So how many are left in *H*?" *There are 10.*

All level IA subjects know how to count up to 15 or more. The answers are of interest in revealing what little use is made of this verbal numeration in their cardinal quantifications, or even in their ordinal quantifications. The reason for this is doubtless that at this level, the numerals "1," "2," and "3," and so on are nothing more than momentary names by means of which the child provisionally distinguishes the homogeneous individual elements in a given collection: "one" is the name of the first discriminated element, "two" its successor, and so on, but no quantitative meaning is yet attached to them. Consequently, when the *n*th element of a whole *T* is being dropped from *H* to *L*, these subjects don't draw the conclusion that the set *T* is divided into two subsets *L* and *H*. They conclude either that everything has dropped, since *n* is part of this whole, or that nothing has dropped, since the only named element (the *n*th) is not yet in *L*. Thus, *Bri* "doesn't know" what is in *H* and *L* after the drops; with *T* = 4 and 3 drops into *L*, she concludes that 4 are left in *H*; after the marbles have been dropped, *Dan* thinks that there is everything (*T*) or nothing in *H* as well as in *L*; when *Cat* is asked to drop 7 marbles, she lets the totality (*T* = 10) of marbles go down, because 7 is included in 10; however, she refuses to consider the 7 marbles as a quantifiable subset because "we can never have 7 with 10." As for ordinal quantifications, the children succeed in counting their successive actions; *Cat*, however, like several others, associates number "one" to the action of picking up the 1st marble and number "two" to making it fall through the pipe—thus, she quantifies as "four" the 3 marbles that have been dropped.

In a word, this first level is characterized by behavior which takes place before quantification. Therefore, our study of the relations between ordinal and cardinal numbers deals more generally with the formation of number as a quantity: In other words, on the elaboration of a system of meanings which are so fundamental that one might have believed them given in the very first experiences with objects, whereas they actually depend upon more complex activities than expected. Thus, at this initial level, an action may well divide the whole T into one subset of "marbles that go" from H to L and a second subset of "marbles that stay" in H, nevertheless the whole retains its meaning as an indivisible object. The parts of this object share the same extension, as if this were a property of a qualitative class and its sub-classes (recall, in another experiment, the example of "flowers" and "daisies" which are also "flowers").[2]

2. Level IB

We include in this level a number of intermediate cases that represent a transition to the establishment of quantitative relations between the number of marbles in L and in H:

ARO (5;9). Situation I, anticipation phase, with $T = 11$: "If we stop before the 5th, where is it?" *In* H. "How many are in L?" *I don't know....4.* "And in H?" *I don't know.* "Approximately?" *Ten.*

Situation II, with $T = 13$: "If we let 10 marbles drop, will the 4th be in H or in L?" *In* H *because they are not put yet. We can't know if we haven't done anything.* Situation II, action phase, with $T = 13$: "You let 10 drop. Where is the 4th?" *It has gone down.* "And the 7th?" *Because I let drop 10 marbles, the seven has also dropped.* "What about the 13th?" *It's in* H. With $T = 8$: "Before the 4th drops, how many are there in L?" *Three.* "And how many in H?" *Eight.* "At the beginning we had?" *Eight marbles. So there aren't 8 any more.* "So how many?" *Five. I didn't count those* (the 3 in L); *I counted only those* (the remaining ones = the 5 other ones).

[2] Inhelder, B., & Piaget, J. *The Early Growth of Logic in the Child.* New York: Norton, 1969.

LAV (5;6). Situation I with *T* = 11, anticipation: "How many before the 5th drops?" *Four* (in *L*). "And in *H*?" *Six, no because it is too close to the 5*. "Then?" *Ten, because it isn't close to the 5*. After dropping the marbles: *There are 9* (in *H*). *There can be 9 or 10 marbles; I thought 9*."

ANA (6;6) reasons partly at level IA when *T* = 11, but correctly when *T* = 8. With *T* = 11, before the 5th marble falls there are 4 marbles in *L*, but 10 in *H*: a little less than 11 or simply 11 minus the 5th. With *T* = 8, there are 3 in *L* (before the 4th drops) and 5 in *H*: *I counted*. "Why didn't you count up to 6?" *Because otherwise there would be 9 in* H (= total number) *and we need only 8 marbles for the game.*

CRI (6;8) distinguishes two subsets as such, that is, the marbles in *L* as dropped and those *which still remain in* H. He counts them with his fingers, but in doing so he continues the counting of the first ones! With *T* = 11: "How many in *L* before the 5th drops?" *Four*. "How did you do it?" *I almost calculated: One, two, three, four, five, and we leave out 1, so that makes 4*. "And in *H*?" *I counted: Five, six, seven, eight, nine, ten, eleven, so there are still 11* (in *H*).

MAR (6;11). Situation I with *T* = 11, anticipation: "How many before the 5th drops?" *There are 5 in* L *if the 5th goes down*. "And in *H*?" *Perhaps also 5: If there are 5, there might well be 5 in* H (symmetry). With *T* = 8, "before the 4th drops?" *Three in* L *because the 3 is before the 4*. "And in *H*?" *I can't know because I don't know the total amount.*

The major advance at this level is that verbal numeration now has the meaning of a quantification which answers the question, "how many?" This enables the subjects to free themselves from the "everything or nothing" reaction which characterizes level IA and to discriminate two subsets within the whole *T*: For instance, *Cri* speaks of the subset of marbles "which go down" from *H* to *L* and of the subset of those "which still remain" in *H*. *Mar*'s final remark clearly indicates a quantitative subdivision of the whole: if the total is unknown, three dropped marbles can be quantified, but nothing can be said of the remaining ones in *H* "because we don't know the total amount." Even though there is real progress, there is a frequent behavior which seems like a residue of the level IA "everything or nothing" reaction: In order to quantify "those which remain," *Cri* (as well as several other subjects) doesn't count them separately but continues counting on from the number of marbles in *L*; thus, once he has given numerals to the marbles in *L*, *Cri* goes on counting "five, six, seven, ..., eleven," for the marbles in *H*; instead of concluding that marbles 5-11 are in H, he infers that 11 remain through falsely identifying "what remains" in H with the whole $T!$ On the other hand, *Aro* starts with the equality $T = H$, and as soon as he remembers that $T = 8$, he can deduce "there aren't 8 marbles any more (in H), but 5," because 8 minus the 3 in L makes 5. Generally speaking, there are still many difficulties at this level when $T = 11$ or more, but the simplified problem with $T = 8$ allows many successes: When *Ana*, who has dissociated the whole $T = 8$ into $L = 3$ and $H = 5$, is asked "why 5 and not 6," she answers "otherwise the sum would be 9 (T in H) and we only need 8 marbles for the game." By contrast, situation II almost always elicits correct answers, attained through anticipation.

3.   Levels II and III

At level II, the two subsets are better dissociated, each giving rise to a separate counting, although there are errors due to counting skill. Here are examples, beginning with an intermediate case between levels IB and II.

SER (7;1) still fails in situation I with $T = 11$. But with $T = 8$ he counts on his fingers the marbles in L (1, 2, 3), and in H (1-5), omitting the marbles which have already gone down, and therefore dissociating the two subsets. "Now is it useful to know that we have eight marbles all together?" *Yes, it helps calculating.* Three batches of two marbles each are dropped. "In which batch was the 5th?" *In the last one.* "Did the 4th fall?" *Yes, because 5 is bigger than 4.*

LAI (7;5). Situation I with $T = 11$: "How many will there be in L before the 5th falls? *Four, and the 5th is still in* H. "What is the total number?" *Eleven.* "How many remain in H?" *Nine.* "Why?" *I counted the marbles* (T), *then I took away the 5 and I found 9* (as if 11 - 5 = 9). Action phase: "How many are there before the 6th one drops?" *Five in* L. "And in H?" *Eight.* "How did you do it?" *I count four in* L, *then I count five, six, seven, eight, nine, ten, eleven, twelve, then I count them* (on the same fingers) *from one to eight.* This is thus not a mere continuation of the counting as with *Cri* (level IB), but an implication that allows the set of ordinals 5th through 12th to have the cardinal number 8.

PAT (7;2). Situation I with $T = 11$: "How many will there be before the 5th falls?" *Four in* L. "And in H?" She counts one to eleven takes one to four, then counts the remaining marbles. *Ah! That's it* (insight), *7 are left!* (by counting again separately marbles 5-11). Action phase: She counts separately one to four in L and one to seven from the 5th to the 11th. "What did you do?" *I know there are 4 in*

L. I count once to get 11: the first 4 (1-4) do not count. I count the other ones again (hence 1-7).

Situation II, anticipation: right answers to all ordinal questions with $T = 15$ and $L = 10$. "How many are there in H?" *It's hard to find out.* She counts 1-15 and then 11-15: *That makes five.*

AND (7;1). Situation II, anticipation with $T = 15$ and 10 drops: He gives the right ordinal numbers. As to the final cardinals, he counts 15 and takes 10, hence $H = 5$.

CLA (8;1). Situation I with $T = 11$, anticipation: *Perhaps there are 8 in H. If we added the 4 that are in L, that would make 11.* With $T = 8$: *Three marbles pass into L, but not four, five, six, seven, eight, ...that makes 5.*

SAN (8;6). Anticipation with $T = 11$: *Four in L and then five, six, seven, eight, nine, ten, eleven. That makes 7."*

Here are now examples from level III (additions and subtractions):

JOE (9;6). Situation I with $T = 11$, anticipation: *Four in L.* "And in H?" *Seven* (subtraction: 11 - 4). "How do you know?" *There are four in L and then I counted* (the remaining ones). With $T = 15$, 10 dropped: "Where is the 10th?" *In L.* "How many are in H?" *Five.* "How do you know?" *Because 10 have been dropped and the sum is 15* (so 15 - 10 = 5). With $T = 8$, 3 of which are in L: "How many in L and in H?" *Three in L, 5 in H.* "How did you do it?" *There are 3 of them in L, plus what is needed to make 8* (so 8 - 3 = 5).

RIC (9;4). Situation I with $T = 11$, anticipation: *There are 4 in L.* "And in H?" *Seven would remain.* "Why?" *Because I did 4 plus 7* (addition), *then I took 7* (from 11: subtraction).

ELI (9;2). Situation I with $T = 11$, anticipation: *Four in L, therefore 7 in H: 4 plus 7 makes 11.*

Situation II with $T = 15$ and 10 dropped. *That makes 5.* With $T = 8$: *Three in L, then that makes 5* (in H). "Show me on your fingers." (He does so.) "Little kids do the same but they say there are 8 in H. What is their mistake?" *Instead of looking on their fingers* (the cardinal in H), *they say the last number they said* (in other words, the last ordinal when enumerating T)!

LAC (9;5). Situation II with $T = 15$, anticipation: *At the end, we have 5 because 10 + 5 = 15. We won't say 6, this would mean we dropped 9.*

The distinct advance of level II over level IB is the clear dissociation of the two subsets L and H within the whole T. The number of marbles in L is easy to determine because it expresses the successive dropping actions, which is an ordination of physical actions whether carried out or only anticipated. Hence, success is achieved at level IB. In contrast, from the nth drop on, the subject goes on with an ordinal enumeration, which is simply verbal or aided by the fingers as a physical support (thus, with $L = 4$, *Lai* says "then I count 5, 6 ... etc., up to the last one"). The novelty of Level II with respect to level IB is that the child understands that "the first four do not count" (*Pat*) and therefore marbles five to eleven must be counted separately: Thus, *Pat* counts again "the other ones" or "the remaining ones" (5-11), in H, but she does so through a new enumeration which, being the sum of elements in subset H, becomes a cardinal one. Actually, this complicated maneuver, typical of level II, is a functional equivalent or a preparation of the operations of addition and subtraction. To say that "the first 4 don't count" (*Pat*) is tantamount to removing them from the whole, and thus to acting out the subtraction. To say "and then" (*Pat*, *San* and others) when going from elements in L to what remains to be found in H in order to constitute the whole T is the equivalent of an additive operation.

Such additions and subtractions are then made explicit at level III. When *Joe* says that "there are three marbles in L, plus what is needed to make eight," the term "plus" consciously denotes addition. When *Ric* says that he "did four plus seven, then took seven," because dropping four from eleven leaves seven (in H), the thematisation of additions and subtractions is equally apparent. Furthermore, we note *Eli's* clarity in explaining the errors occurring at earlier levels by children who, lacking an adequate dissociation of the two subsets, confuse the number of marbles in H and T.

4.   Conclusions

A cardinal number is a set which is conserved in a simultaneous whole, whatever the possible order of enumeration of its elements considered as equivalent units. An ordinal number is [one of] a succession of ranks, each of which is defined by the cardinal number of its predecessors $[n \rightarrow n + 1]$. Obviously, as shown by level II reactions, two mutual implications link cardination and ordination, although this doesn't mean that they are identical, but only that they necessarily depend upon one another: (1) The ordinal implies the cardinal, since the meaning attached to a rank is determined by the cardinal of its predecessor; that is, the nth rank pertains to the element preceded by n - 1 cardinals; (2) The cardinal implies the ordinal because if its elements are equivalent (and they must be considered as such), the only way of distinguishing them is to enumerate them in a certain order.

Therefore, it is only natural that in our experiments subjects make inferences about cardinals from ordinal information, and vice versa. But first, both have to be distinguished. The distinction seems easy to draw, since the ordinals are established through the actions of dropping elements from H to L, whereas the cardinals remain stable either in H (as elements that haven't been dropped) or in L (as elements resulting from the drops). The experiments bring out an interesting fact: Evaluating the number of elements in L is easy because they have been gathered there through actions, but the number of elements in H is problematic because they form a subset $H = T - L$, which subjects attempt to enumerate by merely counting on from the dropped elements. As a result, at level IA there are no implications among ordinals and cardinals (except in the simple sense that n drops imply $\underline{n}$ cardinal elements in L). On the contrary, they are not differentiated, so that dropping a single nth element is believed to entail that the whole T goes from H to L. All the advances from this undifferentiated ("all or nothing") reaction at level IA to the additive and subtractive operations at level III are due to an elaboration of new meanings and of the implications they entail. At level IA, dropping a few marbles represents a kind of absolute, and this is because the meaning is determined by materially performed actions (with no anticipations) which have no relation whatsoever with the whole T or with the remainder in H (on which no action is performed). In contrast, at level IB the drops acquire a meaning of "some" among others, and this in turn gives an unforeseen meaning to the other elements: they are a "remainder," although it is not yet related to a whole.

To give some examples: At level IA, *Cat* says that "we can never have seven with ten," thus refusing the idea of partitioning a set. *Aro* at level IB refers to those which "are not put yet:" This answer includes the new and essential meaning of a "remainder," but one that cannot be known for want of actions performed on it: "We can't know if we haven't done anything." By contrast *Lav* assumes that this remainder must be numerous ("not too close" to the border separating 4 from 5). On the other hand, *Cri* and others wish to count these elements, but they do so only by counting on from the number of drops (hence $H = T$, which recalls level IA reactions). *Mar* invokes symmetry, according to which H "maybe has five" like L. However, the critical change in meanings occurs at level II, when the "remainder" in H is counted separately. There isn't yet a systematic reference to the whole, but the subjects explicitly speak of two subsets: *Pat* says that "the first four (in H) do not count," meaning that they are already known because of the drops; she adds "I count the others (in H) once again" after a kind of insight through which she discovers that the "remainder" have to be considered separately ("Ah! That's it, 7 remain," she says). At level III, at last, the additions and subtractions that were implicit at level II acquire the meaning of operations. As such, they are subordinated to the composition or decomposition of a whole which is constantly invoked by virtue of the basic implications: $T \rightarrow B + H$, or $H = T - B$.

In situation II, the inferences clearly lead to an earlier achievement of implications, as is also the case when situation I is presented with less numerous sets and subsets. All these calculations, even if the subject expresses them through statements, are implications among actions or operations. It is sometimes asked whether every calculation involves some system of inferences: this is obvious if one introduces the notion of action implications.

SECTION II: COUNTING IN A CIRCULAR ORDER

It might be interesting to complete the preceding section by examining how children manage to determine cardinals and especially ordinals when presented with a collection of elements in a circular order. For instance, we shall ask how many buttons there are in a circle containing 10 or 11, then we shall ask how many of them could be the first, the second, the third or the last elements. We may distinguish three levels:

At level IA, the children don't immediately think of marking the element they start with, and their counting ends up with one or two units too few or too many. Above all, they don't see that one may find as many second elements as first ones, and even twice as many if the order is reversed.[3]

---

[3]This statement highlights the concern here with intensions. A second element is part of a sequence—for instance, I may be the second from the right and the second from the left in a row of three persons, and thus be two second elements, at once. (J.E.)

SAN (5;0) counts the elements in a circle of 10 without marking the 1st one and reaches a total of 11. "Which one is the 2nd?" *That one.* "Could another one be the 2nd?" *No.* "Why?" *Because otherwise there is a mistake.* "Could you start counting here (opposite)?" *Yes* (she counts *one, two*). "Can there be another 2nd?" *No.* "And when starting elsewhere?" *Yes, there* (she shows 3 successive pairs [1,2], saying now *one, two,* and then *this one before, that one second*). "How many 2nd ones do you have so far?" *Three.* "Can we find some more?" *No.* "Why?" *Because we haven't counted once more yet.* "Try." She counts disjunct pairs *one, two; one, two*; and so on around the whole circle. Starting again in reverse order, when she meets an element that has already been counted "two," she puts it in the middle of the circle. "How many 3rd ones are there?" (Same procedure.) "How many 1st ones?" *All of them because I could have taken them at first.*

ANI (5;9). The circle includes 7 elements. She counts 8. "No, you counted this one twice. Which one is the 2nd?" *That one.* "If we start here, how much will that make?" *Also 7.* "Why?" *I know* (she counts with another starting point). "Which one is the 2nd?" *There.* "How many buttons can be the 2nd?" (She counts 3 successive pairs:) *Three and also that one* (the 7th). "How many can be the 1st?" *All of them!* (she shows each of them). "And the 3rd?" *Three* (she shows the 3 trios). The experimenter puts 5 elements in a row. "How many elements are there?" *Five.* "And this way" (reverse order)? *It's the same.* "How come that one is the 4th one time and the 2nd the other time?" *Because it is before 5 here.* "And the other way?" *That one is the 4th.*

PAT (6;8) accurately counts the elements in a circle of 11. "How many 2nds?" *That one* (to the left of the first counted element) *and that one* (to the right of the same element): *Two!* "Is that all?" *Five, no 2.* "No, all together (if the starting point is changed)." *Again, 2 of them would be 2nd.* Is that all of them?" *Eight.* "How many 3rd ones?" *Nine!* "And 1st ones?" *All of them.* "And 11th ones?" *Two.* "How come 11 buttons are 1st and only two are 11th?" ... *I don't know.*

In order to better understand the meaning of these initial reactions, let's first examine levels IB and II. At level IB, there is a mixture of understanding with answers resembling the preceding ones:

AND (6;10). He correctly counts the 11 elements in the circle: "How many of them are the 2nd?" *One* (in one direction) *no, 2* (the other way). "Some more?" *Yes, the other way around* (with starting point opposite the 1st). "Some more?" (Two more with new starting points.) "So how many are there?" *A lot* (he counts the pairs as if each element had one 2nd only in the same order of rotation). *That makes 5.* "How many 3rd?" *Four.* "How many 11th?" *All of them! No, only one* (the last one). "And if we count like this" (new starting point)? *Ah! If we change, for each* (term chosen as the 1st) *there is one 11* (insight). "Why?" *Because it turns a little* (i.e., because the first ones and therefore the last ones follow one another in a cyclic order). "How many 3rd ones?" (He doesn't generalize and resumes making triplets:) *Four, no 3!* (with the last 2 buttons). "How come there are eleven 11ths and only three 3rds?" *Because 3 times 4 equals 11. No, because there are only three 3rds* (triplets).

· At level II (7-8 years), these problems are solved. Here are two examples (the first is remarkably precocious):

BRI (5;0). With 7 buttons, he marks a starting point and shows a 2nd one on each side. "Are there some others?" *Yes* (he takes a 3rd "first one" and shows the neighboring elements). "More?" *Yes, anywhere since they are all side by side.* Same answer for the following elements, without separating any pairs, triplets, etc.

HEL (8;10). With a circle of 13: *To count them, we must know where we have started from.* "Could this one (6th) be the 2nd?" *Yes, we can, I started with that one* (the preceding one): etc. *All of them could be the 2nd, but not all at the same time, each in turn because we may start with another side.* "Two of them can't be the 2nd at the same time?" *Yes, but not to count them* (cardinal counting): *We don't count one, two, three, four!* However, to reach the (cardinal) sum, any order can be adopted: *We have the same amount, it hasn't changed.* Ten candies are then laid down on a straight line: *That's 10.* "Can we start elsewhere?" *Yes* (reverse order). "How about here (3rd on the left)?" *Yes* (she marks it). *We count this* (3-10) *then that* (1-2). "Can this one (7th) be the 2nd?" *Yes, we can* (she starts with 6).

At level II, with this experimental procedure, there are clear differentiations as well as mutual implications between cardination and ordination. According to the definitions we recalled at the beginning of Section I-4, a cardinal number is a set which is conserved whatever the order of enumerating its elements. This is what *Hel* asserts when she says that "we have the same number, it hasn't changed." Reciprocally, an ordinal number is [one of] a succession of ranks, each of which is determined by the cardinal of its predecessors. Hence, at level II, n elements will yield (when counting both ways) $2n$ second elements, $2n$ third elements, and so forth. Whereas these meanings and implications are understood from level II on, there is at level IA the nondifferentiation of ordinals and cardinals we noticed in Section I: For a given sum n, the number of 2nd, 3rd, etc., elements isn't $2n$, that is, it doesn't depend on the whole n, but on small disjunct subsets (pairs, triplets, etc.) which are both cardinal and ordinal. This advance in meanings when going from levels IA and IB to level II isn't just a matter of differentiations and mutual implications, but also of a basic relativization of the notions used.

5

RELATIONS WITHIN AN OBJECT

With R. Zubel and G. Merzaghi

The following study may seem trivial because it deals with puzzles of the most elementary kind. However, we must examine what the object concept involves from the viewpoints of meanings and action implications, and for this purpose, the less complex questions are the more instructive ones.

From a general standpoint, the two meanings of an object are, subjectively, what can be done with it and, objectively, what it is made of or how it is composed. The former cannot be separated from the meaning of actions, which we shall not deal with in the present chapter. The latter meaning raises the problem of whether objects are composed from a set of observable properties, or require establishing relations, reconstitutions, and so forth—in other words requiring activities of the subject that are akin to, or even isomorphic to, operations. We wish to show that this is in fact the case, and to do so we shall focus on the simplest questions.

On the one hand, the composition of an object amounts to its properties, which are either observable—even in that case, they require interpretations—or remain to be discovered. On the other hand, this composition consists of the parts or pieces of the object, more or less associated with its properties, and whose spatial connections must be established or confirmed. To elucidate the construction of these various relations, we have analyzed children's reactions to randomly presented pieces of several puzzles. The materials are composed of the following 23 variously shaped cards (see Figure 5):

- Thirteen parts of apples, 11 of which (parts 1 to 11) can be assembled to form 4 complete red apples, with the 2 remaining green parts isolated.
- Five double-sided pieces forming an elephant inside a boa constrictor (*E2-E5*) on one side and a hat (*H1-H5*) on the other. (These illustrations come from Saint-Exupéry's *The Little Prince*.)
- Two one-sided pieces, one a piece of the elephant (*E'2*) and the other a piece of the hat (*H'1*).
- Three pieces that are not part of any puzzle, and cannot be composed with one another or with the other pieces. They represent a piece of a car (*C*), the eyes of an animal (*A*), and a white card (*W*).

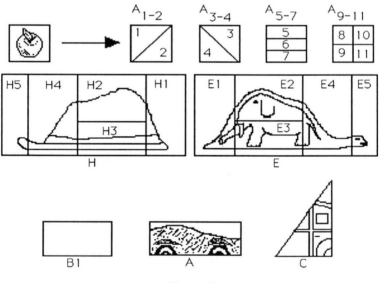

Figure 5

The instruction is simple: "Try to make something and tell me what it is." There is no indication as to the number of pieces to be used. The relations the subject has to establish are either intrafigural (e.g., to reconstitute a complete elephant) or interfigural (e.g., to put the apples together). Our problem is to establish the extent to which these relations have an operatory form: conjunctions, negations, intersections, incompatibilities, implications, and so on.

1. Level 1A

Here are examples from level IA:

TIE (3;5) takes a piece of apple (2). "What is it?" *I don't know.* He puts it together with *8*, also an apple piece but which cannot be spatially coordinated with 2, and he says: *It's an apple; but we must put it here* (end of sheet) *because it's green.* After adding number *6* (middle part), he changes the meaning: *Now I have a house.* He adds pieces of the hat and so ends up with an incongruous mixture which nevertheless has two criteria for near or joined pieces: similar colors and, above all no gaps between the elements. Then he builds up a new set which is composed, from top to bottom, of the elephant's back, the piece of car, a white space, the eyes of the animal, and the piece of a hat (some are laid one upon another): *This is a horse and that is water. It's a horse in water.* Last phase: He joins his two compositions and concludes, *They're only apples.*

AYA (3;1) also starts by coupling pieces (of the elephant, then of apples). Then he gathers 5 of them and he is concerned that they should be contiguous. He shows part of them and says: *It's an apple.* He finishes by surrounding them with a crown of disparate elements, and, very pleased, he says: *A house!*

MIN (3;2). He also begins with pairs or trios of ill-matched pieces and he says each time: *An apple.* Then about another pair of elements, *it is an elephant, a piece of an elephant.* He then piles up a disorderly series of pieces: *It's an apple that falls in the water with the car and a house,* and next he distributes the elements in a line of eight pairs: *They're apple pieces* (in fact, not all of them are); then, *it's a road of apples.* The experimenter points to a pair composed of a piece of the elephant and a piece of apple: "Do they fit?" *Yes, they all fit.*

These 3-year-old subjects (level IB starts at age 4) are interesting because of what is lacking in their constructions. The first randomly chosen pieces are not understood as parts of a total object that should be completed, using one piece as a starting point, and by anticipating the whole of which they would be parts. *Min* is the only subject to speak of a "piece" (of an elephant), but he never looks for the other pieces, either by prediction or by trial-and-error: They are merely associated to new ones until such "pseudo-totalities," composed of heterogeneous elements, give rise to meanings. These meanings have the following features: (1) They can change in the course of construction: After new additions, *Tié*'s "apple" stops being one, for "now I have a house" (see also *Aya*); (2) They refer to temporary situations and not to permanent objects: "It's a horse in water," says *Tié* or, as *Min* says, "an apple that falls in the water with the car and a house" or "a road of apples" including pieces of the elephant and of the hat. Furthermore, *Min* states the general and essential feature of level 1A when he asserts that "they all fit." That is, anything fits with anything providing that one invents an arbitrary link, instead of seeking the link through anticipation, finding it through a necessary conjunction, or justifying it objectively by relating observable data.

2. Level IB

From age 4 on, there is a remarkable turning point in this search for the object: The initially selected puzzle piece, whatever it may be, is used as a "referential" element that is to be completed in order to produce an isolable and preservable object characterized by "intra-objective" relations. Such relations are "constrained conjunctions," achieved partly through empirical trials, and yet in equal part through local anticipations, whether accurate or erroneous, and which to various degrees guide the subject's search.

MAR (4;1) starts with *E'2* (back and eye of the elephant) which she couples with the neighboring part, and says, *it's a fish.* Then she picks up piece *4* (half-apple) which she correctly composes with piece *3* (the other half), and she says: *It's an apple.* Then she takes *A* (eyes of an animal), looks for a matching piece, and concludes correctly, *There isn't any.* She looks again among the *Es* (parts of elephants): *No, there is something missing here.* She goes back to the apples with a green piece: *I'm going to make the green apple.* She gathers the pieces and notices that they are not spatially suited to each other. *That doesn't work, because it goes too far here, and also there.*

FRE (4;6) starts with a piece of apple (2) and says: *It looks like a tomato.* He tries to couple it with *4*: *It's not the right one* (i.e., the complementary part). In the next six attempts he repeats: *It doesn't work; It doesn't work either;* etc. He ends up with a correct combination of 5, 9, and 11: *It's all done. I think it's an apple. I'm going to look for another one.* He discovers that *2* goes with *1*, then *3* with *4*, hence three apples are completed through negations and intra-figural conjunctions. Then he turns to the elephant and succeeds in matching *E2* and *E3*, saying *we must leave them* (as they are). However, (referring to the remaining pieces): *nothing works* and he conjectures that *someone removed a picture* (a piece). He gathers these negative elements in a separate group which reminds us of $p \cdot q$ in the incompatibility, $p \setminus q$!

FRI (4;2). He identifies, at the outset, several possible apples in pieces *1* to *11*. He makes different pairs, then he compares *E2* and *E'2* and concludes: *I've got three apples and two animals.* For *H4* and *H1*, correctly oriented but joined together: *It's a snail.* "Are you done?" *No.*

GAR (4;2) brings *E2* near *E'2* but says, *No, because there are* (that makes) *two whales.* "And that's too many?" *Yes.* However, for *H1* and *H'1*: *That's one caterpillar going up and one going down.*

AMA (4;5). Starting with *7* as a reference element, she succeeds with *7, 8, 10*: *This is an apple and one there also* (in other combinations). As to the *E*s, the experimenter proposes substituting an *H* for an *E*: *That fits almost as well.*

CAR (4;9) successfully couples *8 + 10* with *9 + 11* and then assembles another apple (*5 + 6 + 7*): *It's finished and there too.* As to the elephant, he gathers *E2 + E3 + E4* then correctly adds *E1*: *I've got all the pieces* (except *E5*). Then he completes the figure and recognizes one half of a *snake* (the boa constrictor) and then, *the second half.* However, he thinks the elephant is *the other half* of the hat.

There are substantial differences between these 4-year-old subjects and the 3-year-olds at level IA. The major one is the formation of intraobjective relations based on spatial contiguity, that are conserved by means of "constrained conjunctions"—even when the objects are cut in pieces and must be reassembled in closed and stable wholes. In other words, these subjects don't construct heterogeneous sets such as those *Min* imagines when he sees "an apple that falls in the water with the car and house," concluding that "they all fit." Instead, these children start with a figure they rightly suppose to be a piece of apple (for instance), and use it as a reference to assemble the object with complementary pieces. This results in the generation of new and basic actions with the following mutual implications: (1) A search for "constrained" conjunctions that will lead to the total object; and (2) a necessary and correlative emergence of exclusions or negations. As an example of the latter, let us quote *Fre* when he is looking for "the right part" to fit against the reference element. *Fre* successively rules out six pieces while repeating each time "it doesn't work," "it doesn't work either," until he relates parts *5, 9* and *11* and says, "it's all done; I think it's an apple." He then goes on to assemble two other apples, thus integrating with the intraobjective conjunctions others which are interobjective and even "inclusive" (with respect to the class of apples).

Besides those basic advances, we notice several others. *Fre* is not satisfied with partial negations and he gathers the unused pieces into a separate class: "With those, nothing fits." Further, although these subjects don't start their projects by anticipating the final shapes, they become capable of partial inferences as soon as they begin a construction. We must note, however, that the relation between the two images H and E remains an unsolved problem. The children either establish a few connections within H or within E without investigating their interconnection, or they believe the two patterns can be synthesized: For *Ama*, the substitution of an H piece for an E piece only gives rise to the judgment that "it fits almost as well." *Car* states a belief shared by subjects looking for the relation between H and E: Set H makes up "the other half" of set E.

3. Intermediate cases and level II

The tasks are so easy to solve that, once the basic pre-functors[1] are formed at level IB—these take the form of conjunctions constrained by intrafigural contiguities and by exclusions or negations—further advances are mainly of a procedural rather than a structural nature. At this point, anticipations of the object under construction become quicker and more complete, several reference elements are used, transfers from one construction to another increase, and so on. Only one structural problem is left, a highly interesting one as we shall see. This problem is whether the two sides of H and E (hat and elephant) are related in the sense that *Car* views them as two "halves" of a single totality, or whether they are independent images, as in a picture book where there is no relation between

---

[1]In category theory, a *functor* is a generalized function that maps the internal structure of one category to that of another. Piaget's notion of *pre-functor* undoubtedly refers to an analogous cognitive construction by which the internal features of distinct objects can be related, compared, and transformed. In this passage, Piaget alludes to connections between the present project and other recent work. See Piaget, "Structures et Catégories," *Logique et Analyse*, 1974, *17*, 223-240; Piaget et al., *Epistemology and Psychology of Functions*, Dordrecht: Reidel, 1977; Piaget, *Recherches sur les Correspondances*, Paris: PUF, 1980; Piaget, *Morphisms and Categories: To Compare and Transform*, Hillsdale, NJ: Lawrence Erlbaum Associates, in press. (P.M.D.)

the front of a page and its back. Accordingly, solving this problem is our main criterion for distinguishing level II from level IB.

To begin with, here are some intermediate cases between levels IB and II:

TRI (6;8). At the outset, he takes *E1, E2, E3*, anticipating the total object, and completes it. Then he picks up *5* and says, *it's the stem of an apple*. He takes *9* and *3*, but puts *3* back: *It doesn't fit*. He assembles *8, 10, 9, 11*: *It's all done!* He thinks that *H4* and *H1* make up *a hat*. But, after mixing *Es* with them, he sees an elephant. After further attempts with *Hs* and *Es* he can conclude only that *some pieces are missing*.

ERI (6;1) quickly assembles the apples. He anticipates the elephant, which he constructs quickly, except for *E5* which he views as *a snake*. As for the *Hs*, he had previously identified *H2* as *a mountain* and *H3* as *a bridge, a river*, and therefore the whole as *a landscape*. After having built *E* he wants to build the *H* again but notices that *pieces are missing*, without remembering he had turned them over, and he concludes: *You took the other piece*. Thus, he doesn't understand that the opposite sides involve two independent systems.

CEC (7;7) mixes up *Es* and *Hs*. When the experimenter suggests turning them over, she ends up with *an elephant that isn't finished* and a *hat that isn't finished*.

Here are some clear cases from level II:

IAN (7;5) identifies three reference frames (apple, elephant, hat) and distributes the corresponding elements in three respective collections. Then he assembles the apples, and *an elephant* with *E2 + E3*. He makes *a mountain or a volcano* with *H4 + H2*, but when he wants to complete it, he only finds *half a mountain and half an elephant*. After observing that some pieces have been "removed," he turns a piece over and exclaims, *Ah, now I know: There was an elephant and you turned it over*. To his utter surprise, he discovers that the mountain appears when turning over the elephant, and he puts the pieces in correct order.

GRE (7;8) succeeds immediately in assembling the four apples, then he says of *E2, E5* and *E1*: *It's an elephant game*. He picks up *H3*, turns it and composes it with the *Es*. Next to *H4* he puts *E1*, turns it over to show *H1* and says: *It's a kind of head*, which he completes with *H4* and *H5*: *Ah, it's a turtle: The head is there (H5) and the hump is there (H2)* "What will be on the back side?" *The elephant!* Thus, he obtains two independent systems each of which he assembles correctly: *It's done!*

OLI (8;11). After the apples, he takes *H4* and discovers *E4* on the other side. He assembles the *E*s correctly. Can you make something else? *Yes, maybe if I destroy something.* That is what he does with the *E*s, discovering that *there is something like that on the other side*, and he arranges the hat: *So now I have the hat, and then afterwards the elephant.* He turns the pieces of the hat, one at a time, and checks that he finds a well-arranged elephant.

DID (8;3). After the apples, he takes *H5, H3*, and *H1*, and *E1, E2* and *E4*, and says, *right now they're all halves.* He predicts *a hat* and, *Also halves of an elephant: they are halves that can't be put together!* Then he discovers that *before those weren't there* (H4 and H2); *perhaps they were on the back.* "So what can we do?" *Turn them.* He systematically turns the pieces one by one.

NIC (8;10). For *H4 +H1*: *It's a hat*, which she completes with *H5*. Then she assembles a few *E*s: *It's already a piece of a snake.* As the hat is *not very well done* and as the elephant is incomplete, she turns the pieces over one at a time and understands the duality and yet the separateness of the two systems.

The 10- to 13-year-old subjects, who are at level III in other domains, have quicker anticipations and inversions than the children just cited; although, in comparison with adults' reactions, theirs are much more variable. There is no indication of new structures here but merely procedural variations.

We can establish from the level II reactions that only at about age 7-8 do children understand that a drawing on the reverse side of a card might be unrelated to the drawing on the first side. Before reaching this age, they either mix *H*s and *E*s and conclude that some pieces are missing from the complete image, or they suppose (like *Car* at level IB) that one half of the object is on each side, as if the elephant formed "the other half" of the hat. The problem here is therefore one of meanings.

Indeed, in addition to the duality between meanings of objects (an apple, etc.) and meanings of actions (to unite or to dissociate, etc.), we must further posit the duality of that which is signified and that which signifies. The signified here are either the objects represented by the picture cards, or actions that can actually be carried out. Signifiers can be either words (or morphemes), arbitrary symbols (such as the signs representing addition, multiplication, and other mathematical operations), or images whose only meaning is to represent objects external to themselves. From much earlier studies[2] we know that in young subjects, the object and its verbal signifier are not differentiated: In other words, the name is part of the object (for instance, one need only look at Mont Blanc or the Salève to know what they should be called). In the present case, and before level II is reached, the external object and its drawing or image are seemingly also undifferentiated: On the back of a card representing an elephant, one must find a part of this object or a related element (even if it is a hat), as if an image were a real object that could be turned over to see another side of it. At level II, on the contrary, what is found at the back of a picture is another picture that is independent and forms a complete system of its own.

In addition to such an essential structural advance, level II is characterized by numerous procedural improvements. Anticipations are quicker and a better guide for constructions because they immediately aim for the final form of the object. Frames of reference are more numerous, so that subjects simultaneously use one of them for the apples and others for the elephant and the hat. Very often, the children distribute the elements into three groups before beginning detailed constructions. Their constructions may give rise to transfers. Finally, proximal negations (e.g., pieces which are useless for E but useful for H or vice versa) are extended into distal exclusions or negations (entirely useless prices).

4. Conclusions

The two general goals of this book are to find where one must start to construct a logic of meanings and to show that such a logic is based upon implications and other relations among actions and operations.

In no way can a logic of meanings be limited to a logic of true or false statements. It must pertain to the referents of statements, and therefore to objects themselves, as is the case in the present chapter. As noted previously, the meaning of objects has two aspects: (1) First of all, it is "what can be done" with them either physically or mentally. Physically, one can—or cannot—move an object, separate it into parts, and so forth. The meanings of objects are thus subordinate to meanings of actions. What can be done mentally is to classify or seriate objects, and so on, which again subordinates them to meanings of actions or operations. (2) The meaning of an object is also "what it is made of," or how it is composed. Here again,

[2]Piaget, J. *The Child's Conception of the World.* Littlefield: Adams, 1972, pp. 63-70. (Original work published 1926)

objects are subordinate to actions, which moreover are constructive and
not merely utilitarian.

Actions exist and function only through their interrelations, and this
is as true for elementary as for sophisticated actions. The most general
interrelations are the implications between actions or operations, of which
there are many examples in this chapter. The following are the most
frequent: (1) breaking a picture into pieces implies the possibility of some
adequate means of reconstituting it; (2) assembling some pieces implies
excluding others; (3) configurations of pieces imply "constrained conjunctions" (of the form $AB \rightarrow A$ in Anderson and Belnap[3]), such that A
cannot be separated from B, and so forth.

In addition to these operatory connectives (implications between
actions and "constrained conjunctions" linking the parts of an object), we
also observe in this study what we may call "free conjunctions." These
arise when the pictures represent a complex object whose elements are not
always associated in the real world, such as the elephant in the boa
constrictor. Boa constrictors do not actually swallow elephants and,
surprisingly enough, even subjects who are unfamiliar with *The Little
Prince* are not particularly bothered by such an unusual combination. We
may also identify a third type of conjunction, which we shall call "interobjective" or "inclusive" conjunctions. These consist of uniting in a single
collection objects which are composed in different ways but share the
same meaning, as when subjects speak of "four apples" from level II on.

Furthermore, we can identify four types of incompatibilities: (1) There
is an "intraobjective incompatibility" when two similar objects (e.g., two
apples) are dissimilarly decomposed such that a piece resulting from one
decomposition cannot fit together with a piece resulting from another.
(2) The incompatibility is "interobjective" when joining parts of two
different objects (e.g., an apple and a hat) is impossible. (3) There is a
"complete incompatibility" when the pieces presented or chosen fit with
nothing and form a class (such as the intersection of apples, elephants and
hats); this may be compared to $p \lor q$ in the classical formula:

$$(p \cdot \bar{q}) \lor (\bar{p} \cdot q) \lor (\bar{p} \cdot \bar{q}).$$

(4) Finally, we shall speak of a "presentative incompatibility" when two
objects drawn on opposite sides of a cardboard (e.g., an elephant and a hat)
may be composited, yet can never appear together simultaneously. These

[3]See chapter 11 and the General Conclusions.

latter cases necessitate adding the operation of spatial or infralogical "inversion."

A closely related connective is simple reciprocal exclusion, or "neither...nor" ($p \cdot \bar{q} \vee \bar{p} \cdot q$). Although it is probably as frequent as incompatibility, it differs in the use and meaning of negation. This is an essential question from the standpoint of the logic of meanings: In an extensional logic based only on truth tables, the negation of p which occurs in the implication $p \supset q = (p \cdot q) \vee (\bar{p} \cdot q) \vee (\bar{p} \cdot \bar{q})$ refers to everything that is not p in the universe of discourse while maintaining the truth of q. From such a negation come the paradoxical implications[4] which must absolutely be avoided. Whereas in a logic of meanings, negation only occurs with respect to a well-defined inclusion. For instance, in a grouping where $B = A + A'$, the meaning of the negation of A in the expression $A' = B \cdot A$ is relative to the inclusion of A in B. Therefore, it is advisable to distinguish "proximal negations" which refer to the closest inclusion from "distal negations" referring to ever more distant boundaries.

We shall now review and try to explain the evolution of exclusions or negations through our developmental stages. The evolution is roughly from the seemingly more primitive distal negations to proximal negations, which become progressively refined with increasing age. The reason for such transformations lies in the transformations of the reference frames themselves; however, we first need to be clear about the two senses in which we have used this term. On the one hand, we have used it in the sense of inclusions, with respect to which certain conjunctions are either possible or excluded. On the other hand, when describing developmental levels, we have spoken of a "reference element" to designate an invariant piece with respect to which conjunctions of other pieces are organized. At level I, children use only one reference element, so that there are relatively fewer elements available to complement it and relatively more that must be excluded. This is what makes the negations distal. By contrast, level II children simultaneously use several reference elements, corresponding to apple, hat, and elephant. Consequently, their negations become more and more proximal, since the three systems must be completed separately as well as jointly.

From a general standpoint, therefore, the negations used serve to index degrees of difference. In a previous study with B. Inhelder[5] we had

---

[4]See chapter 11.
[5]Piaget, J., & Inhelder, B. *The Early Growth of Logic in the Child.* New York: Norton, 1969.

also noticed that proximal negations are rather late: For instance, a subject said that "A stone is *more not* a daisy than a primula is," and the words "more not" of course meant that there is a greater difference between a stone and a flower than between two objects that are both flowers.

To the various preoperatory connectives already discussed, we must add "equivalence." When there are four ways of decomposing and reconstituting an apple, obviously there is an equivalence, not only among the resulting objects but among the procedures, each of which aims to avoid discontinuities at the various connecting points and to make well-shaped round apples. Although non-exclusive disjunctions and intersections are not explicitly constructed by the subject, we may notice implicit ones. For instance, the apples the subject is assembling may be divided in two classes through interfigural links (see Figure 5): If p = apples which have less than four subdivisions ($\{1,2\}$, $\{3,4\}$, $\{5,6,7\}$) and q = apples which have more than two subdivisions parts ($\{5,6,7\}$, $\{8,9,10,11\}$), then the apple with three subdivisions constitutes the common part ($p \cdot q$) of these two classes, as opposed to the two other parts ($p \cdot \overline{q}$ and $\overline{p} \cdot q$).

To sum up, our subjects employ connectives that are isomorphic to 10 of the 16 future binary operations. The six remaining connectives are tautology, complete negation, and the affirmations and negations of p or q (i.e., $p \cdot q$, $p \cdot \overline{q}$, etc.). The 10 that are used are all connectives between meanings that do not depend on an extensional truth table. Extensionality only intervenes in partial inclusions governed by meanings and their "inherences."

6

INTER-OBJECT NEGATION AND INCOMPATIBILITY

With L. Banks and A. Wells

The relations among subdivisions of objects we described in chapter 5 pertain both to the intraobjective domain (concerned with composition of objects), and to that of "infralogical" connectives (characterized by properties such as neighboring, continuity, and separation). These are quite separate issues from those of the logico-arithmetical domain of relations between discrete objects, where the wholes involved are classes or collections and not continuous objects with interconnecting parts. In both cases we naturally find that forms of conjunctions, exclusions, implications and incompatibilities characterize the subject's activities. But are they actually the same, and do they evolve in an analogous way at the various levels of development, especially with respect to actions or preoperations and their meaning implications? The main difference is that, although it is difficult to see "pieces of objects" in nature apart from the subject's separating actions, as soon as one subject has made such a separation, another subject can perceive at once the incompleteness of each piece taken by itself and thus can perceive its negative aspect. In contrast, confronted with two classes A and B and a third one C (neither A nor B), subjects look for the shared positive features of C before observing that there aren't any and accepting that Cs are nothing but "neither A nor B." Therefore, it is useful to return to the problems of negation and incompatibility at the interobject level.

SECTION I: NEGATION

We have already studied negation on many occasions, but never with the following experimental procedures, which provide us with some new information. In the first procedure children are shown an object and asked everything this object is not or "everything we cannot do with it" (recall that one of the meanings of an object is "what can be done with it"). Accordingly, the reference frame for the negation is decided by the child. Alternatively, children are presented with about 10 objects, and asked to designate one of them and tell what this object is not, which may lead them to use the whole set of objects as a reference frame. Taken separately, each of these two questions is of course inadequate, for the former (approach) may well only give rise to verbal productions, and the latter to successive exclusions in action without any preliminary attempts at classification.

Therefore, we have devised a second, more precise procedure. A screen separates the child from one of the experimenters. Various objects are placed before the child, who chooses one of them. The experimenter must figure out which object it is according to information provided by the subject, but this information must always be negative (i.e., the child must tell what the object is not). For instance, if there are two red marbles and a horse and the child chooses the latter, it would suffice to say that the object is neither red nor a marble for the experimenter to deduce that it is the horse. Then they change roles: the experimenter provides the information and the child draws the conclusions.

The third procedure is to ask the child to classify the objects in collections, each of which, once constructed, must have a name. Then the experimenter asks if one object in a collection *A* can be placed in a collection *B*. Subjects who answer "no" are asked why not. If the answer is "yes", they are asked if the name for the collection must be changed and what it should be called. Finally, a new and quite different object, which we will call "the intruder," is inserted in the collections and the child is asked if "it fits well" with the other objects and to explain why or why not.

1.   Level I

To begin with, here are a few examples from level IA:

HEL (3;9), presented with a pen: *It's a pencil.* "What is it not?" *Nothing at all.* "What can we not do with it?" *I don't know.* "What can we do with it?" *Mark on a sheet.* "How about that (a rhombus)? What is it?" *A kite.* "What is it not?" *It has no string.* "What can we not do with it?" *Nothing at all.* "What can we do with it?" *We pull and we run with it.* (An incomplete circle is presented.) *It's a broken bracelet.* "What is it not?" *There is nothing at all; it's all alone.*

Using a screen with roles reversed (2 cars, 3 animals, 1 marble): "It's not a car and it's not an animal. What is it?" *An animal and car.* "But I tell you it's not an animal. What is it?" *An animal and a car.* "But I tell you it's not an animal and it's not a car, so what is it?" (She shows the whole:) *It's all that.* "But what did you choose?" (She shows the red car and then the pig.) With the 'intruder:' *Everything fits well together* (including the 'intruder:' a chocolate among fruit).

MAT (3;9). A ballpoint pen, two felt pens, a fountain pen, an eraser, and some paint brushes are presented. "What is that?" *A pencil.* "Can you tell what it is not?" *I don't know* (in spite of the frame of the reference formed by the 7 objects.) "What else is there?" *They're all* (!) *pencils.* "What can we not do with them?" *We're not allowed to draw on the walls, on the table or on the scissors.* "What is this (eraser)?" *Round.* "What is it not?" (No response.) "What can we do with it?" (No response.) "There is nothing to say?" *No.*

Screen: complete failure. Exchange of roles: "If I tell you it's not a wooden object and it's not an animal, then what is it?" She shows a sheep but also the plastic car (correct).

NEV (4;4) asserts that a pencil is not a pencil, then that a pen is not a pen. With the screen: She successively shows all the objects without taking negations into account. Exchange of roles: "If I say that it is not blue?" *That one because it is blue.* "It is not a fruit." (She selects the pear.) "It's not a pear, not an orange, not an apple." *It's the orange.* When she tries to find a name for a set of objects, it doesn't apply to all the elements: The collection called "animals," in addition to the horse and the pig, includes a marble and a prism. Obviously negations are misunderstood because of the problem with inclusions.

SON (4;6) is unable to classify the objects in collections and she assembles somewhat heterogeneous pairs, such as an accordion with a telephone. About the pen, she says: *It's a pen.* "I would like you to tell me what the pen is not." *It's not a pen.* "But you just said it was a pen." *It's not a pen, that's a pencil.* "So is it a pencil?" *Yes.* "But what is it not?" *It's not a pencil, nor a table, nor a chair, nor spectacles, nor a man* (these objects are on the table).

We notice with *Son* some initial negations with visible reference elements, and thus the emergence of level IB. Here are some further examples of intermediate cases (IB) between level IA and II:

JEA (4;6). A rhombus is presented: "What is it not?" *A triangle.* "What else?" *There is nothing else.* With the incomplete circle: *It's not a square and not a triangle...I can't think of anything else.* The ballpoint pen: "What isn't it, or what can't we do with it?" *We can't make a house.* "We can't draw a house?" *Right.* "And, what else?" *It's not a bear, not an elephant, not a cuckoo*, etc.

With the screen: *It's not a tree, not a house*, etc. (he enumerates all objects except the one he has chosen). Exchange of roles: *It's not a car and it's not an animal.* "What is it then?" *It's a car.* (The screen is removed; same negations by the experimenter:) *It's a car.*

DEL (4;3). With a rhombus: "What is it not?" *I don't know ...It's not for talking.* (With screen and changed roles:) "It's not an animal and not a car." *You chose the sheep.* "It's not an animal?" *Yes, it is.* (The screen is removed and the dual negation is repeated.) *It's a sheep.* With 'the intruder:' correct answers.

SEV (4;0). With a rhombus: "What is it not?" *Not what?* "No, what is it not?" *That.* "Is it a car?" *No.* "Then?" (No response.) Incomplete circle: *It's the head.* "What's it not?" *The body.* The pen: "It is not...?" (No response.) "What can I not do with that?" *Write.* "We can't write?" *We can write.* "So what can't we do?" *A balloon, a fir tree*, etc. With the screen and with roles changed: "It's not a car and it's not an animal." *It's a sheep* (Screen removed and negations repeated:) *It's a ball* (correct). "It's not green and it's not a man." *It's the telephone* (correct). With the 'intruder:' The answers are right at first, but several heterogeneous objects *all fit well*, due to the lack of hierarchized inclusions.

At level IA, there is a failure with all negations: The child cannot discover what an object is not; when told that the object chosen behind the screen is neither *x* nor *y*, the child concludes that it must be an *x* or a *y*, and so on. This deficiency respecting negations goes with two systematic gaps or defaults in the construction of inclusions and in the significance of the expression "everything fits together well," which is explicit in *Hel* and *Sev* and implicit in all the other subjects. The first characteristic flaw is to introduce into a collection elements which do not belong in it, for instance to put a marble and a prism in a set called "animals" (*Nev*). The second and closely related error is to confuse a whole with one of its parts, as when *Mar* says that seven heterogeneous objects "are all pencils." In both cases, there is a confusion between the whole and the parts, or between extension and intension. This amounts to confounding "free conjunctions" (by means of which a few objects have been assembled) with "constrained conjunctions" which are based upon shared meanings that unite "what fits together well" into a class with common features.

Consequently, at these elementary levels we can identify an initial type of conjunction that is neither the later acquired "constrained conjunction" (e.g., to put a pig and a horse together because both are animals and as such cannot be separated), nor the "free conjunction" (e.g., between a ninepin and a bird because they are neighbors in a spatial arrangement—an extensional criterion independent of intensional meanings, and one that permits the elements to be separated). We shall call such a conjunction a "pseudo-constrained conjunction," by analogy with the "pseudo-necessities" we studied in previous investigations (and which are characterized by a confusion of the general with the necessary).[1] At level IA, subjects may introduce into a collection given to them, or which they have constructed themselves, a set of "pseudo-constrained conjunctions" of various degrees, which vary according to the materials presented.

We now have a better understanding of the paradoxes of negation. When children are told: "It's not an animal and it's not a car," they infer that the two sets are being specified because they constitute pseudo-constrained conjunctions with respect to the neighboring elements: Hence affirmation prevails over negations due to this special mention. Similarly, when children sometimes say that an object is a pencil, and sometimes that it is not a pencil, this is because the object may have a varying role according to the elements with which it is compared: It will be a pencil if it is related through a pseudo-constrained conjunction, but not if the connective is a free conjunction.

Briefly, the difficulty of negations at level IA is due to the poorly structured conjunctions inherent in the idea "what goes together well," and therefore inherent also in the beginnings of inclusions. Indeed, inclusions have multiple and contradictory meanings, from mere heterogeneous gatherings with free and arbitrary conjunctions, to sets based on pseudo-constrained conjunctions of various degrees, and eventually to classes based on common properties (e.g., "animals"). Lacking stable and sufficiently differentiated reference frames, exclusions or negations cannot have general meanings. Therefore, negation is difficult because it presupposes two successive phases: (1) Constructing a possible conjunction between an x and one or more ys (otherwise nothing can be said about it, as *Hel* affirms about the incomplete circle: that which "it is not" reduces

---

[1]Piaget, J. *Possibility and Necessity, Vol. II: The Role of Necessity in Cognitive Development.* Minneapolis, MN: University of Minnesota Press, 1987.

to "nothing at all," because "it is all alone"); (2) Negating this conjunction. In other words, to say that *x* "isn't blue" means that it could be blue,
and if the subject conceives of the conjunction as "pseudo-constrained,"
he favors "what could be" and ignores negation. The advance at level IB
is an improvement of inclusions, hence there is an advance in negations
mixed with level IA errors.

2. Level II

At this first operatory level, inclusions become consistent and provide
negations with reference schemes that extend rapidly to distal negations.

JOE (7;3). In the task using 'the intruder,' he classifies separately the three
kinds of fruit, then, when chocolates are added, he classifies all the elements as *fruit
and chocolates*. When a ninepin is added, the whole is distributed in two classes:
What we can eat and what we can't eat.

FAB (7;6) mentions more than 12 objects to designate what the pen "is not."
In the situation involving the screen, he leads his partner to the chosen object
through easily formulated negative expressions, and succeeds just as easily when
they change roles. He formulates only one irrelevant negation, *It's not made of
iron*, but at once acknowledges that this negation is useless.

GIA (8;10). Same reactions. He starts by saying, *It's not a balloon and it's
not a car*. "Do you think that's enough?" *No. It's neither a dog nor a roof* (prism).

BOR (8;6). A pen *is a thing that isn't like us* (persons) and pens *are not
animals*. To classify the objects, he reasons in terms of *families*: The green sticks
are gathered together because *they belong to the same family*, which is also the case
with the wooden figurines, but not with the telephone and the eraser. Using the
screen, he responds to "it's not green, not brown and not a person" correctly with
it's the cow. In another trial, he correctly sees that the information is insufficient.

SYL (9;11). With the screen: She points to the objects and says, *For instance,
if it's neither people nor a tree, then it would be the telephone*. She chooses the fir
tree: *It's not light green and it's not people*. "Is that enough?" *No, she could say
it's that* (telephone). *We must say: It's not green and it's not a person*. With roles
changed and using red objects, two animals and one ninepin she reasons as follows:
They're neither red, nor animals: What is left is only the ninepin.

LOR (10;3). With the screen: "Could you say three things so that the other person may guess" (among green sticks, a red prism, a fir tree, and a horse)? *It's not green, it's not rectangular and it's not an animal.* "Then it's the red prism." With a balloon, a red doll, the prism, a telephone and a whistle: *This time you can say just two things—It's not red and we cannot blow in it.* "So it's the telephone." *Yes.*

The advance in the construction of inclusions (or "families," as *Bor* says) leads not only to a correct use of negations, but to two noteworthy new abilities. First, the subject can discriminate (as *Syl* does) information that is sufficient from information that is not. This presupposes a possible partition of inclusions into coordinated subsets. The second innovation is that the situation involving the screen is as easy for subjects when they must formulate negations about objects as when, after changing roles, it is the experimenter who provides the information ("it is neither an *x* nor a *y*, etc."). The curious contrast in this task informs our observations regarding the general difficulty in finding and using negations prior to level II. When the participants change roles, the experimenter provides the negations and the subject only needs to deduce their consequences. Yet, at level II, children generate negations as easily as they infer their outcomes. This progress must be related to what we just said about recognizing sufficient or insufficient information, and this explains why younger subjects have greater difficulty with producing sufficient negations than with using those provided by someone else.

SECTION II: INCOMPATIBILITY

We have already dealt with incompatibility[2] and we shall come back to it later, so we will limit our discussion to the main technique used in the present study. The child and the experimenter each have a deck of cards. The cards in one deck represent animals, and in the other, plants. The animals include four quadrupeds, four birds, four insects (including a caterpillar), one snake, one eel and one fish. The plants include four flowers, four fruits, three vegetables, two mushrooms, two ferns, one lichen, and two algae.

The children are given the animals and the experimenter holds the plants. First, the children are asked to make a spontaneous classification

---

[2]See chapter 5.

of their cards—to put together the cards that go together. Then they are asked to name the classes they have composed. Once this first part of the procedure is completed, the experimenter classifies his own cards according to the criterion of incompatibility: He makes a pile of all flowers, a pile of all fruit, and a pile with the remaining cards. The children are asked to name each of the piles, and finally, to make a similar classification with their own cards and to give a name to the piles they have constituted. Three levels of response will be distinguished.

3. Level I

Here are examples of level I (4-6 years):

NEV (4;4) only puts together heterogeneous pairs (fish + spider, etc.); but, after seeing the adult's three classes, she also makes three piles: (1) a *pile of pigs* (pig, ants, dog and spider); (2) *a pile of dogs* (donkey, fish and 2 birds—the label refers to the donkey); (3) another *pile of dogs* (the remaining elements). When she is shown that there are no dogs in 2 and 3, she adds a goat in 2, keeps the name *pile of dogs* and calls 3 the *pile of birds*. Again we find the previously mentioned confusion of parts with the whole (*pars pro toto*) at this level.

SON (4;7) makes four piles, each including a bird and only one that is homogeneous (the snake and the eel). In response to the adult's demonstration, she just counts the elements so as to make piles with the same number of elements. Hence, she has three piles, each of which (like *Nev*) she names after only one of its members.

CAR (5;2). Same reactions. He is shown the adult's model and explicitly told, "Here are the flowers, here are the fruits and there is a pile where there are neither flowers nor fruit. Do you understand?" *No*, he replies.

SYL (6;7) shows a clear advance through his classification into 5 piles: *Insects there, everything that crawls here, everything that flies here, everything that lives in the water here, and there, everything that runs fast*. Nevertheless, he doesn't understand at all the interviewer's proposed pattern, despite the designations, "Flowers there, fruit there and the rest there."

These initial reactions shed light on the kinship between negations and inclusions. To unite objects because they have common features (constrained conjunction) implies excluding those which do not have these features, and reciprocally, negation is meaningful only with respect to an inclusion (or inherence of meaning). As the subjects do not succeed in constructing such collections (and as they name their collections after one member instead of expressing their common meaning), they do not understand what principle lies behind the experimenter's model and do not conceive of collection *C* as being negative, although they are told that it is neither *A* nor *B*. In other works, they do not view *C* as a result of "free conjunctions," as opposed to *A* and *B* which result from constrained conjunctions based on common meanings. On the contrary, they attribute to *C* "pseudo-constrained conjunctions," corresponding to those we dealt with in section I while analyzing the difficulty of negation. In spite of the differences in experimental procedure and in questions asked, there is therefore an instructive convergence here, which adds confidence to our interpretations. Furthermore, recall that the confusion between parts and the whole observed here in subjects' labelling of their collections also appears in the field of numerical relations. We frequently observe subjects at this elementary level who believe that ten units removed from a set of thirty or forty make more than ten units taken away from a set of twenty.[3]

4.   Levels II and III

Level IIA is characterized by operatory inclusions, and the subjects try to define class *C* (neither *A* nor *B*) using various inclusions. They do not achieve the negation "neither *A* nor *B*," although they sometimes approach it by defining *C* as "the others."

> *JAN* (6;7) ends up with three classes: *A*, Animals with two legs; *B*, animals with four legs; and *C*, *those which have many legs.* "Does the fish have many legs?" *I put them outside* (i.e., they cannot be classified).
> *AND* (6;8). *It's difficult to give a name because there are many things.*
> *CLA* (7;0). Class *C* is *the rest*, the *others.* Hence a difference but not yet a negation.
> *JOE* (7;3). Class *C is all combined* (= mixed up).
> *DAV* (7;4). *The fruit, the flowers and* (*C*) *the things that grow.*

[3]Inhelder, B., & Piaget, J. De l'itération des actions à la récurrence élémentaire. In P. Gréco, B. Matalon and J. Piaget, La formation des raisonnements récurrentiels, *Etudes d'Epistémologie Génétique*, vol. 17. Paris: P.U.F., 1963.

FAB (7;6). *Those that don't go together* (i.e., they don't form subclasses of a single class *C*).
RIC (8;6). *Those with hair, the birds, and the others.*
SAI (8;6). Class *C* is *everything for eating, we could put it on meat.*
JUL (9;5). *It's all mixed up.*

Restricted by the instructions to making 3 classes *A*, *B*, and *C*, these subjects do not achieve an explicit negation (*C* = neither *A* nor *B*), although they can see very well that *C*s are incompatible with *A*s and *B*s. They instead limit themselves to exclusions in action, which produce three kinds of reactions: The first of these is to try to find a common quality for all *C*s comparable to that of the *A*s and *B*s. For example, "having many legs" (*Jan*), "things that grow (*Dav*), and "things for eating" (*Sai*). The second reaction amounts to saying that *C* is "all combined" (*Joe*) or "all mixed up" (*Jul*) or "those that don't go together" (*Fab*), the latter implying that these items would have to be distributed in subclasses comparable to *A*s and *B*s, and hence a belief that more than three classes are required. The third reaction is the closest to the dual negation "neither *A* nor *B*," and consists of calling *C*s "the others" or "the rest" (*Cla*, *Ric*, and others). In a sense, this is a dual negation, but expressed in terms of positive "differences" instead of explicit negations.

Not until levels IIB (9-10 years) and III is the common property of the *C*s explicitly thematized in a negative form, "neither *A* nor *B*:"

DID (8;2). *A = Insects. B = Those which have no legs. C = They are not insects and they are not those which have no legs.*
COR (8;5). *C = The non-birds non-insects*; that is, neither *A* nor *B*.
MAT (8;6). *C = What is not the insects (A) nor things that fly (B).*
JOA (9;3). *C = Animals with no hair and with no feathered wings.*
ICA (9;10). *C = Animals which do not fit with those (A and B).*
LOR (10;3). *C = Those which are not birds (A) and not insects (B).*
MIR (12;2). *C = We may call them 'neither flowers nor fruit.' It's a bit long but it's OK.*
PIE (12;5). *C = We may call them 'neither flowers nor fruit;' and, in the case of animals, 'not insects and not reptiles.'*

In comparison with the present results, solutions to the problems in section I show a delay in achieving explicit incompatibility, especially when the screen is used. This is apparently because when deducing the chosen object in section I subjects start with given or initially constructed negations of the form "it is not x, y, z," and so on; whereas, in the present problems they start with positive inclusions (As and Bs) so that "the others" can only be characterized through the dual negation "neither A nor B." Hence the search for a common property of the Cs, during which labels such as "the others" or "the rest" actually mean "those which are still to be classified." Later, the expression "neither A nor B" is accepted as sufficiently descriptive, although it is still less decisive than the negations given in the situation involving screens in section I.

7

WEAVING

With G. Piéraut-Le Bonniec and E. Rappe du Cher

This investigation uses two looms consisting of wooden frames (25 cm wide and 50 cm high) to which ribbons (2 cm wide) are fixed vertically as warp threads. Light-colored ribbons (rose, yellow, and orange) alternate with dark-colored ones (purple, dark blue, dark green), in the following sequence: rose (r), purple (p), yellow (y), blue (b), orange (o), green (g). White (W) and black (B) ribbons are used as woof-threads that go alternately over and under each warp-thread. The white ribbons are used for the odd rows and the black ribbons for the even rows.

If row 1 starts with the intersection W/r (a white ribbon over a rose ribbon), the series of overlaps in that row will be W/r; p/W; W/y b/W; W/o; g/W (see Table 1a). A second row is formed by introducing a black ribbon. The row alternation is reversed so wherever in row 1 the white woof lies over the warp and hides it, the black woof goes under the warp and makes it visible (see row 2 in Table 1a). In row 3, a new reversal of the alternation restores the pattern in row 1 as the system is cyclic. As Table 1a shows, the weaving thus obtained presents the same light/dark alternation going across each row, forming a pattern of columns. Table 1b shows the design that obtains if instead of having the first white ribbon go over the rose ribbon, one starts by having it go under it: a light/dark alternation downward, forming a pattern of rows.[1]

To investigate the subjects' representations of this system, they were given small cube-shaped magnets. These were of four colors: white; black; beige to symbolize the light color ribbons; and brown to symbolize

---

[1]To master this situation requires constructing two systems of meanings. The first one refers to objects, that is, the ribbons. The subject must understand that there are two categories of ribbons (the warp and the woof) whose relations are either necessary or impossible: e.g., *B/W* or light/dark is impossible; but *(W* or *B)/* (light or dark) is necessary. The second system of meanings refers to the actions that are performed on the objects. Two forms of these should be distinguished.

The first form is concerned with the rows. One action implication of this type involves alternations: If the ribbon goes under the warp, it must be brought back over the warp and so on reciprocally. Another refers to reversals: If row 1 starts with *W/r*, then row 2 starts with *r/B*.

The second form is concerned with cycles. Repeating the reversal produces an alternation in the overlaps at the beginning of each row and creates cycles. It is thus possible to predict the overlap of two ribbons at any point in the loom: If the row is an even one, for each warp the overlap will be like the corresponding overlap in row 2; if the row is odd, it will be like that of row 1. However, this alternation may be reversed because *W/r* and *r/W* are both possible at the beginning; consequently, we have implications such as the following: If one starts with *r/W*, then *l/W*, *W/d*, *B/l*, *d/B* will be the four crossings obtained.

Clearly, solving the problem completely requires a fair number of action implications. The question is whether subjects working on the loom necessarily abstract the meaningful organization of the ribbons, or master all the action implications of both types. (G. P.-L.B.)

The two patterns, columns and rows, can be visualized with the aid of graphic representations of the warp and woof ribbons shown below. (J.E.)

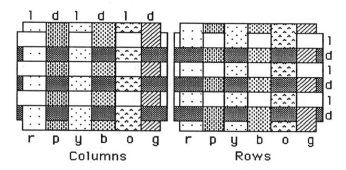

Columns   Rows

Table 1. The Two Inverse Patterns.

1a. Pattern of Columns.   **1b. Pattern of Rows.**

$$l \ d \ l \ d \ l \ d$$

First row: First row:

(Above)	$W \, p \, W \, b \, W \, g$			$r \, W \, y \, W \, o \, W$	(Above)
(Below)	$r \, W \, y \, W \, o \, W$	l:		$W \, p \, W \, b \, W \, g$	(Below)

Second row: Second row:

(Above)	$r \, B \, y \, B \, o \, B$			$B \, p \, B \, b \, B \, g$	(Above)
(Below)	$B \, p \, B \, b \, B \, g$	d:		$r \, B \, y \, B \, o \, B$	(Below)

Possible crossings:

The light columns:	$W \, l$	The light rows:	$l \, W$
	$l \, B$		$W \, d$

The dark columns:	$d \, B$	The dark rows:	$B \, d$
	$W \, d$		$l \, B$

Key.

Warp		Woof
l = light	d = dark	B = Black
r = rose	p = purple	W = White
y = yellow	b = dark blue	
o = orange	g = dark green	

the dark color ribbons. When stuck together, the cubes can be used to represent the four kinds of overlaps in each model.

The procedure is as follows: First, the children are shown the column pattern already woven and are told to look carefully at the way the ribbons are placed. They are then given a loom on which only the warp-threads for the same pattern are attached, the task being to insert the correct woof-threads. The subjects' behavior in the following six subtasks is evaluated:

1.   Introducing the first woof ribbon so as to produce an alternation. If the child makes mistakes, he or she is corrected in order to proceed with the next step.

2.   Introducing the second woof ribbon so as to create a reversal.

3.   Introducing the third woof ribbon, which completes the first cycle.

4.   Anticipating the kinds of overlaps: The positions to be filled by the white and black ribbons are marked on the left and right sides of the wooden frame, and subjects are asked to predict the overlaps of warp and woof at given points on the loom.

5.   Carrying out the reverse pattern: Subjects are shown the row pattern and are asked to copy it on the unused part of their own looms.

6.   Representing the two inverse patterns by the four overlaps that define each of them: Given the small magnetic cubes, the children are asked to demonstrate how the ribbons cross in each of the two patterns.

The reactions of 20 children from 4 to 12 years old were recorded on video-tapes. Their solutions permitted establishing three levels with some sublevels.

1.   Levels 1A to 1C

Here is an example from level IA:

RIC (4;3) formulates a nice implication: *The white one goes under this one because we find it on the other side.* He can assert that the models are different and can show the local differences between two neighboring woof ribbons, but he cannot carry out a correct alternation on his own empty loom. Nevertheless, he declares: *We do it underneath and then over.* "If we keep on doing the same thing?" *It falls down, but if it's underneath and (then) above it doesn't fall.* He still makes mistakes, however, and finally says: *The W and the B are not the same: The W is made to be put underneath.* Following his rule he tries the whole *B* ribbon underneath, then makes corrections.

And from level IB:

RAP (4;7) succeeds in placing the *W*s on her loom: *Once there* (under *r*) *and once there* (over *p*), etc. "Are you sure?" *Yes, because it was like this* (on the pattern). "How about the *B*s?" *It's exactly the same as the *W*s (in fact, she places them the same way as the *W*, seemingly because she lacks inversion: *B* under *r*, then over *p*, etc.). *They do the same thing.* "Is your *W* like the *W* on the pattern?"

Yes. "And your *B*?" *No, there is something that goes wrong.* She makes a local correction, thus creating an error in the alternation of rows (two *B*s without a *W* in between). She tries to start all over again, but actually repeats the same pattern with the error in alternation, which she cannot combine with the inversion.

LAU (6;1) cannot immediately distinguish the two patterns. He starts with columns: *They* (the *B*s and *W*s) *must be played the same.* To predict a remote overlap, he must carry out all the intervening ones.

And from IC:

EME (6;3) finally makes the inversion and alternation compatible, but only after numerous errors: Three successive *W*s over *p, y,* and *b*; and the *B*s placed like the *W*s. He fails at representing the pattern with the magnets. His conclusion: *We must do it all over again because now I know how.*

In sum, this level I (A to C) is characterized by a minimal number of inferences and by a collection of local and empirical copies of particular aspects of the models. "I did like this with my finger as if it was the ribbon," says *Eme*, while indicating either alternation or inversion, but without combining them inferentially, and achieving synthesis only after various errors. In other words, this level is one of successive actions, linked together only in a post-hoc fashion, and bereft of explicit action implications. Consequently, there are no anticipations accompanied by an understanding of "reasons," nor are reasons sought be the subjects.

2. Level II

From about age 7 or 8, various explicit inferences appear with the use of terms such as "because" (reasons) and "then" (consequences). Hence, our interest lies in implications both between actions and between conscious meanings. Although they do not yet constitute a structured whole which would be formulated as such, implications are already inserted in a system of relations that are understood successively. This system is akin to a double grouping, which includes the seriation of intersecting threads and the classification of alternating colors *l* (light) and *d* (dark).

Here are a few examples from level IIA:

TIZ (5;2) initially fails at alternating the *W*s, then copies the overlaps one by one. He has the same problem but then succeeds with the *B*s. Immediate success for the second pattern (rows).

GIN (6;9) also succeeds with an alternation of *W*s, but then he weaves the *B*s similarly. "Is it all right?" *No, because I did it like the* W*, and it is not the same color.* Then he succeeds in combining *W*s and *B*s vertically into columns, and makes successful predictions, although after several corrected errors. He gives a good classification of *l* and *d* colors using the magnets. "Can we have *W* over *d,* then *W* over *l* in the same game?" *Yes...No.* "Why?" (No response.) "And *B* over *l* followed by *B* over *d*?" *No, yes.* "Show me where on the loom." *No, we don't have it.* "Why?" (No response.) "What then?" (He corrects it to have *d* over *B*.)

GAN (8;11) points out the difference between the two patterns and chooses the one with columns. He correctly places the *W*s. "Are you sure?" *Yes, that's good because there it goes over, while there it goes under and there over.* "How about the *B*s?" He correctly positions the first *B*. Nevertheless, to anticipate a remote intersection, he has to construct the intermediate states, taking into account the alternation of light and dark colors *B* over *l*, etc. For instance, he notices *d* over *W*: *Then next, it's going to be* B *over* d. But he ends up with *B* over *l* and *d* over *B*; then *B* over *l* followed by *B* over *d*; then a correction to *d* over *B* and other local changes which prevent him from organizing the whole system. "If we start with the *B*, shall we find the same rule?" *No, that will change the rule.*

Here are examples from level IIB:

BER (6;6) makes a good reproduction of the two series. "If I put *W* over *l* do you think I'll get something new?" *I think they are already there* (he shows them, correctly). "Is it possible to do the contrary?" *No, because in that game, it's the* B *that passes over the yellow one* (light). "And if we lay down the magnets like this (*l* over *W*, *W* over *d*, *l* over *B* and *d* over *B*)?" *That isn't right because it's impossible for them to be like that in this game.*

TAM (8;6) also generalizes this relation: *It's like this in the game. Look, the* B *is always over a light color and always under a dark color.* "If I already have those two (*l* over *W* and *W* over *d*), can we get *B* on *l*?" *No, because I don't see it on the pattern. It's not possible to have the* W *and the* B *over the light ones, otherwise we would need two light ones side by side.* An exchange is proposed of a *W* over *d* in one series for a *d* over *W* in the other series: *It's not possible on a loom, I don't get it.* Thus, what *Tam* can do with the magnets prevails over what he sees on the looms.

Level II is characterized by a gradual transition from empirical and local copies of the pattern (level I) to a tentative control of the whole system and its structural laws, hence we see a mixture of observations and inferences that relate them through action implications. At level IIA, some successful predictions are observed, but they only occur after corrected errors, whereas in IIB there are justifications in forms such as: "It's always like this in the game" (*Tam*); "It's not possible on a loom" (*Ber* and *Tam*). Therefore, there is a search for the "reason" why this follows that, but it is limited to a reference to the specific model rather than the intrinsic conditions of weaving. However, from what they discover while manipulating the magnets, level IIB subjects get closer to these deeper reasons.

In a word, level II is a transition from what was at level I only an essentially empirical copying endeavor, with all the errors and omissions of an exogenous way of understanding, to what will become at level III an endogenous understanding of the "reason" for laws and generalized empirical facts. This behavioral progression amounts to supplementing and almost replacing the initial physical knowledge of observables with a logico-mathematical knowledge of the structures involved. In simpler terms, it is the construction of a "deductive model" which is indispensable for understanding the proposed systems.

In this respect, the magnets play an important part as means for the construction of such models. At level I, they have no other meaning than adding a new problem to those already generated by the two patterns. At level II, they acquire the meaning of symbols that permit a more general and more simplified modeling of the overlaps. With such an instrument, level III subjects will reach what is only sketched at level II: an effective and general understanding of the relations involved in the looms. Although these relations are gradually generalized at level II, they don't yet exhibit any intrinsic necessity.

3. Level III

At this last stage, the subject is not only able to deduce the relations involved, but also justifies their necessity and therefore seeks and establishes "reasons:"

> *PAT* (10;4). At the outset, he succeeds in carrying out the alternations *because if the* W *passes over one color, the* B *must pass under the same color.* Predictions of remote crossings are correct: *Here the* W *will be above because it always passes over the purple, so that's required, as we can see with the other white we have already done.* With the magnets, he puts W over *l*, B over *d*, *d* over W and *l* over B. "Could we make another series?" He produces *l* over W, *d* over B, W over *d* and B over *l*. "And if we want to do a third series?" *We could start with the* W *over*

the light colors and under the dark ones; and with the B *over the* d *and the* W *over the* l. "Is this a new series?" (He looks at the alternations:) *Ah, yes! It's the same as the first series. We can only make the two series we have already made.*

ROB (10;6). Correct alternations with one local error corrected immediately. "How did you notice you had made a mistake?" *I compared with the* W: *It's got to be the other way.* "When you get to this point, how will they be?" *The* B *will be under the orange thread.* "Why?" *I take my bearings on the yellow thread.* With the magnets, he arranges two groups of three elements each: *B* over *l*, which is above *W*; and *W* over *d*, which is above *B*. Such compositions express a true understanding of the structure. "Can we have *W* over *l*?" *No, that cannot be done.* "And if I put *l* over *W* and that *W* over *l*?" *It depends on the number of rows: That would be possible with an even number, but here we've got nine rows.* "Now, on the same loom, is it possible to have the *W* going over *l* and under the *l* as well?" *Oh no, because there is always a dark thread in between.* "And an *l* over a *W* and also *d* over a *W*?" *No, that's not possible: They would have to all be over or all under.* "Could we make exchanges between the two series?" *That's not possible, because if the* W *is over the* l, *it can't be over a* d.

AUD (12;0). About the woof ribbon *B*2 with an anticipation of the remote overlap: *We can know by looking on the same line: For instance, the* B *goes under the orange thread, so we know it's got to go over the green and under the rose. We could also just look at the white thread, since all whites go the same way.* He makes a complete listing of the various reference elements that might be useful in predicting an overlap. When the interviewer proposes an exchange between two series of magnets: *We couldn't put them in that one (column) only, because if one (of the sets) has a* W *going over a dark color, then the light color couldn't go under the* B. *That would be the opposite pattern* (i.e., in the situation with rows).

XYS (13;0) goes so far as to propose only one pair of magnets to generate all possible overlaps. Symbolic thinking is developed to such a point that he proposes several series of pairs which cannot be found on the same loom. *Yes, if we wanted him to play this game* (columns), *we would give him only* l/B *and he would know how to go on.* "How?" *Yes, one is enough, since we know that light colors go over the* B; *we also know that dark colors go under the* B, *and so with the* W *it has to be the other way around.*

What is new in such answers is that inferences are not restricted to arguments such as, "it's always the same because it's like this" or "it's impossible because I don't see it in the game." Instead, necessity, possibility and impossibility are motivated by deductions which provide their "reasons." In particular, the magnets become general symbols, and their combinations constitute "explanatory models" which can be applied to the looms, and even enable the subject (as with *Xys*) to construct all possible combinations.

4. Conclusions

The general evolution we have just outlined develops gradually from coordinations among literal actions—whose meanings are not entirely brought out even when the movements have been performed—to coordinations of inferences whose meanings are imposed in their anticipations. This doesn't prevent some general implications being formulated, beginning with level I, which determine all further actions. For instance, "the *W* goes under (this warp ribbon) because we find it on the other side" (*Ric*). As for the detailed actions to be performed in reproducing relations belonging to a specific pattern, it is noteworthy that younger subjects need to perform them through movements of the hand or fingers before turning to the ribbons and making them follow the path that has been discovered through the action itself.

This general evolution of course includes some discrepancies, such as the greater ease with which children manipulate the magnets than they do an entire loom. Nevertheless, we have verified a basic progression from the coordination of actions to inferential compositions, where the manipulations are directed by reflective abstractions.

The more specific interest of this study is that it bears on a complex structured whole whose various features are interdependent and are hard to identify at first sight. The tree structure described in chapter 2 represented a structured whole that was easier to discern since all the partial paths were based on the same dichotomous links. Here, on the contrary, we are faced with separate relations (alternations of the *W* or *B*, inversions, multiplicity of the overlaps, correspondences with the magnets, etc.) which are related through a very complex structured whole that is understandable only after detailed analysis. We must therefore make a distinction between two kinds of action or meaning implications: *Local* implications which pertain to a single relation (alternations of *W*s or *B*s, inversions of *W*s and *B*s, repetition of overlaps, etc.); and *systemic* implications which unite the local relations into a consistent whole and provide "reasons" for it. From this viewpoint, our three levels clearly represent a progressive construction of systemic implications: Lacking at level I, they start at level II (although limited to "reasons" of the type, "It's always like this in the game"), and finally dominate at level III, where the intrinsic "reasons" for the system are understood.

Accordingly, the action implications at level I are of the "local" type, and the meaning of actions is determined by their observed outcomes on the looms. Only in rare exceptions is an implication deduced without any empirical control, as when *Ric* declares (and is even sure) that if the *W*s or the *B*s were always over or always under they "would fall down," which doesn't happen when there is an alternation. That such an alternation may be continued indefinitely is both an inductive inference and an observable fact.

At level II, the first systemic implications appear in comparison of patterns, or judgments about what is possible or impossible on the looms. As already pointed out, however, the inferences do not reach necessary "reasons," since the only reasons consist in claiming that certain relations are "always" or "never" found in the cases observed, which indicates a confounding of necessity with generality. Even so, such reactions demonstrate that there is by now a "system" for the subject, instead of merely a collection of local regularities. It is only at level III that systemic implications prevail to such a point that *Xys*, for instance, is able to deduce all the other possibilities from a single pair of magnets, which indicates the victory of the "necessary" over the "general."

Finally, let us notice that even from the first level the children establish relations that are isomorphic with respect to future operations. Alternations are what we call "constrained conjunctions," or conjunctions of terms that cannot be separated; whereas the warp ribbons lead to "free conjunctions" (i.e., there is nothing compulsory in putting the purple thread beside the yellow one, since only the *ldldld* series is necessary). Inversions constitute a kind of negation. Exclusive disjunctions define the relation between *B* and *W*, and we may speak of a non-exclusive disjunction when *W* over *l* entails either *B* over *d*, or *l* over *B*. There are also incompatibilities, and so on.

8

THE MEANINGS OF COLLECTIONS

With A. Henriques, D. Maurice and V. Jacq

This chapter is divided into four sections, of which the common theme is the construction or transformation of collections representing seriation or classification structures (i.e., groupings).

SECTION I: MODIFICATIONS IN A SERIATION
With V. Jacq

The procedure of this first study is quite simple: Once a seriation of nine variously sized nails has been laid out vertically, subjects are asked to point out and to describe the "middle-sized" (i.e., the fifth) element (*M*). They are then asked what can be done, using a supply of nails, to change this "medium-sized" nail into "the biggest" or "the smallest."

1. Level I

Subjects belonging to the first level, IA, find various solutions:

XAV (4;5) picks up a smaller element to replace the medium-sized one. He declares that *We must pull it like this*, and he shows how to lengthen it at both ends, indicating that length is not conserved.

FRE (4;6) takes the largest nail and places it in the middle of the seriation. He notices, however, that this disrupts the seriation, and he only says, *I can't do it.*

CAR (4;4). For the middle-sized element to become the biggest, she is content with saying that its position *must be changed* and she places it at the beginning of the series, before the bigger ones. To turn the medium-sized element into the smallest, she places it at the other end, after the smaller ones. "What did you do?" *I've changed places*—as if once she has constructed the right series with size determining the places of the big, middle-sized, and small elements, the places themselves should confer size on the other elements.

ERI (4;10) replaces the medium-sized element by the largest one, which he lays down obliquely so that it links the other elements which form two separate vertical orders: *It has eaten and grown a little bigger.*

AND (5;6). In order to turn the medium-sized element into the largest one, she exchanges their respective positions, and does likewise with the smallest nail to make *M* the smallest. Then the nails are mixed up and she is asked to change a medium-sized element into "the biggest of all." She lays it down beside a small one, which in her opinion, is enough to give *M* a new size.

DAR (4;11) lays one of the largest elements on top of the medium-sized one to lengthen it, or one of the smaller ones on top of *M* to "shorten" it.

JEN (6;6) places the biggest nail on top of *M* to lengthen it. To shorten it, she places the smallest element at one end of *M*—as if this didn't also lengthen it, although a bit less.

DAV (6;0) constructs the whole series in one vertical line and places *M* at its peak. To make *M* smaller, she merely replaces it by the smallest of all. "And to make it medium-sized again?" *We must keep it medium; otherwise it won't be medium any more.*

None of these children understands the very simple action of removing the elements larger than *M* to render it the largest of all, or of removing smaller elements to make *M* the smallest of those that are left. In other words, these reactions are not compositions of relations but are limited to what we may call *coupled predicates.* The most frequent among them consists of just "changing places," as *Car* says, and of putting *M* at the beginning or the end of the series, as if position determined size and not the reverse.[1] For some children, such a change in position acts materially on *M*, changing its real length: "It has eaten and grown a little bigger," says *Eri*. For others, the element must be pulled at both ends when the change of position is carried out, which also indicates an absence of length conservation (*Xav*). For others still, a neighboring relation with large or small elements is enough to modify *M*, even if it is placed beside the seriated elements and not within the series (*And*). *Eri* divides the series into two vertical columns, linking them with an oblique *M* which is thereby supposed to become the longest of all. Other subjects are content with lengthening *M* by laying down a large element on top of it (*Dar* and *Jen*).

In a word, despite an initially correct seriation there is no operatory composition of the relations involved; these are instead replaced by semi-relations consisting of coupled predicates based on the general relation "to fit with."

At level IB we meet similar behavior, but it includes corrections leading eventually to a new solution: To dissociate the 1-9 seriation into two series so that the first one (1-5) includes *M* as its largest element and the second one (5-9) includes *M* as its smallest element.

AVI (4;3) starts with level IA reactions, then makes a non-seriated alignment of elements with a relatively large *M* in the middle. To make it "the smallest," he then merely lays it down horizontally, with all other elements remaining in a vertical position. Nevertheless, he reaches the right solution when he seriates all the elements and separates the seriation into two partial series 1-5, 5-9 in which *M* fulfills the two conditions of being the smallest in 5-9 and the largest in 1-5.

KAT (6;0) also proceeds by trial-and-error, but as soon as the experimenter separates series 1-5 and 5-9, he understands that the element which was formerly *M* becomes *the smallest* compared to the large ones, and *the biggest* of elements 1-5. Further, it *is also the medium-sized one.*

ARC (6;4) destroys the seriation to make *M* larger than some other elements, and then smaller than the remaining ones. Thereupon he discovers an astute solution: He arranges all elements so that they form a roof with *M* as its summit, which makes it bigger than the lateral elements while keeping its position as a medium element (with 3 nails on its left and 3 on its right). However, there is no solution for *M* as the smallest element.

[1]In other words, in this example the predicate *position* and the predicate *size* are "coupled" inappropriately through pseudo-necessity (cf. chapter 6, p.75). (P.M.D.)

BID (7;11). At the outset, he removes the large elements which makes *M* the largest of the remaining ones. He does likewise with the smaller elements: *We remove everything, this one stays and it's the smallest. No, it stays all alone* (laughs), *this doesn't work.* He goes back to the level IA solution with *M* beside the smallest element in the series. Then he finds the correct solution when he removes either the large elements or the small ones from the seriation, so that *M* becomes the biggest or smallest. But he expresses this outcome in terms of coupled predicates.

KAR (7;6) also starts with level IA solutions, then he constructs a roof and analyzes it in terms of coupled predicates: *Next to this one, it has shrunk; next to that one, it is the largest.*

Therefore, level IB is a transition level leading from coupled predicates to composable relations. This transitory nature is apparent in solutions such as the building of a roof, which compromises the seriation by splitting it into two ascending and descending slopes without any horizontal base.

2. Level II

At 7-8 years, the solution is found at once by eliminating the bigger or smaller elements so that *M* becomes the biggest or the smallest while remaining the medium-sized element in the whole series.

SAC (7;10). He starts by declaring the solution *Impossible: In every case it will remain as it is.* Then he splits the series and shows that *M* is the biggest in one of the two new series, the smallest in the other and the middle-sized one in the complete series.

CEL (8;6). *We only have to remove those (1-4) then* M *becomes the biggest and this one* (new middle-sized element) *will be the new middle-sized one.*

NAT (8;1). *In there* (initial seriation), *it's the middle. We remove this* (the bigger ones) *and* M *is the biggest. If we remove this* (the smaller ones), *it is small.* "And if I place it at the end (of the complete series)?" *Then it's still the middle one.*

FLO (8;10). *In order to make it the biggest we only have to remove the bigger ones.* "And to make it become the smallest?" *We do the opposite.*

3. Conclusions

These findings help to elucidate the role of the meanings of predicates and of compositions themselves. We can distinguish three kinds of predicate meanings:

(1)   "Coupled predicates" which are indissociably linked, such as the size of an element and its position in a seriation—as if changing an element's position entailed simultaneously changing its size (level IA).

(2)   A more refined linkage is to think that putting a large element next to some small ones, or vice versa, modifies the size of elements that have become neighbors, through a kind of contagion.

(3)   The predicates are eventually relativized: The terms "big" and "small" are meaningful insofar as they relate to reference frames and are thus essentially relative: Big means "bigger than x" and small means "smaller than x." This evolution in the meaning of predicates cannot be separated from a transformation in the mode of coordination, which starts as a mere figural arrangement and ends as a composition of relations proper, the latter indexing the arrival of concrete operations (level II). In other words, the evolution of meanings corresponds with a development of action implications, which do not constitute pure "forms" but depend directly on the nature of their contents.

SECTION II: THE MEANINGS AND INTERNAL REASONS FOR
COLLECTIONS
With A. Henriques and D. Maurice

4.   Classifications of Variable Elements

With B. Inhelder, we have formerly done extensive studies on the formation of classifications.[2] At that time, we restricted ourselves to the simplest of procedures: Children were given a number of objects and were asked to arrange them as they wished, without adding or suppressing elements in the course of the experiment. In what follows, we seek to extract the meanings and relations involved in the details of such behavior, and in particular we wish to analyze children's reactions as we introduce successive modifications of the set of objects to be classified.

[2]Inhelder, B., & Piaget, J. *The Early Growth of Logic in the Child.* New York: Norton, 1969.

The materials include two large white candles, three medium red candles, five small blue and white striped candles, and seven spherical yellow candles. The following variations are performed and the subject is asked, for each modification, how to name or characterize the set of elements:

1a: The children observe the interviewer place one of the large white candles in a box. The box is closed and they are asked what should be written on a label to indicate its contents.

1b: Then the box is opened and a medium-sized red candle is added. The children are asked if it is necessary to change the labelling: If so, they dictate to the experimenter what must be written on the new label. The procedure is the same for each addition to the contents of the box.

1c: A small striped candle is added.

1d: A round yellow candle is added.

The procedure is then repeated by removing items in the reverse order:

1c: A round yellow candle is removed.

1b: A small striped candle is removed.

1a: A medium-sized candle is removed.

(In order to determine if the mode of presentation plays a part in the attribution of meanings, two conditions are administered, one group of children starting with the increasing order, and another group with the decreasing order.)

2a: The subject is presented with two large white candles in the box and is asked for a label.

2b: Two medium red candles are added.

2c: Two small striped candles are added.

2d: Two round yellow candles are added.

(The same procedure as above is then followed, removing two candles each time in the reverse order.)

3a: One large white candle and 1 label are presented.

3b: Three medium red candles and 1 label are added.

3c: Five small striped candles and 1 label are added.

3d: Seven round yellow candles and 1 label are added.

(Then, as in the two previous situations, one type of candle is removed each time. In all situations, one group of children starts with the increasing order, the other with the decreasing order.)

We have determined three levels. The first (4-6 years) is characterized by the use of absolute predicates with no relational connotation. The second level (6-9 years) is characterized by an insertion of elements into partial classes which themselves are not grouped as sub-classes in the total class. Finally, a complete hierarchical grouping[3] appears at the third level (10-12 years). Note that if complete success appears somewhat late on this task it is because of the adjoining and deletion of elements: Such groupings with varying contents are harder to elaborate than groupings whose contents do not change and which therefore have stable sub-classes. With the usual experimental procedures, the latter appear as early as age 7-8. This enhances the value of the present procedure, since it multiplies the meanings, inferences, and action implications involved.

Here are examples from level IA:

TIE (3;7) agrees with the fact that the objects are candles (however, he calls them *pencils*) and that the round ones are also candles which can be lit. "What is it?" *Balls that can be lit.* But when he is asked to name one set in a box, he restricts himself to an enumeration: *A blue pencil, no a white one, a red one, a pencil with white lines* (= the already named blue one). "Could you find one single word for all that is in the box?" *Yes, two white pencils, two pink ones and two little ones.* "But, what if we put all of them together?" *A tree, it looks like a tree.* "Could you make two piles by putting what goes together well in each?" (Through one-to-one correspondence, he makes two identical piles.)

MAR (4;1) also enumerates the contents and, for two sub-classes (two boxes) he also establishes two identical sets by a correspondence. "Could you say in one single word what is in the box?" *Pink ones, blue ones, yellow ones, and white ones.* Furthermore, the large white candle is defined as "white" throughout the experiment regardless of context.

At level IB, the reactions are the same, except that an object may have two conjoined predicates, which are still absolute:

SIM (5;2). "If I take both together?" *White ones and white ones.* "If I can't see them, how will you describe them to me?" *White ones, but one is small and the other big.*

From level II, small disjoint classes are constituted and relations among predicates are established. Size will thus have three degrees: big, medium and small. On the other hand, the same object may be defined according to its color, size or shape. In particular, the "round" and "long" candles make up two classes, although no generic term yet exists:

[3]See chapter 2, p. 19, footnote 1. (J.E.)

TOI (5;5) starts naming the sets according to the number of elements: *There are two candles here and one there....We have four there and that's all,* and so on. But he comes to size and discriminates three small classes that may be seriated: "What do you call them?" *One that's big, three are small and five even smaller.* When the subject divides the candles into two heaps, one of them is composed of *the fat ones, the medium ones and the small ones,* and the other of *all the round candles.* There is no identity or one-to-one correspondence between the heaps, as was the case at the preceding levels. The whole set gives rise to a first generic term: *Box all full of candles,* but as soon as one of them is removed, *Toi* reverts to enumeration.

JOS (7;6). She starts by labelling through an enumeration of contents. "In one single word?" *We can write 'candles.'* "And if you make two piles?" (Without any hesitation she gathers the round ones in one heap and the rest in the other:) *The round ones are there and the long ones there.*

CAR (7;4). Same initial labellings as *Jos.* Then she is asked to construct some series which go well together. She makes five groups, which are seriated according to color and size: Three bunches of round candles according to color and the other ones according to size.

STE (8;0) arranges the sub-classes: *By colors.* "Could we do otherwise?" *Yes, by sizes.* "How about the whole?" *Candles of all colors.*

Level II is halfway between disjoint classes and comprehensive classes, the subjects most often preferring the former. We accordingly notice a relativization of predicates, which has two consequences from the viewpoint of action implications. On the one hand, affirming a predicate entails relating it to similar ones through a "constrained conjunction." On the other hand, noticing differences leads to differentiating new subclasses. The whole construction of operatory "groupings" then consists of an equilibrated synthesis between similarities and oppositions. This synthesis is well under way as early as level II, but it is only completed at level III. Here is an example from this last level:

FRA (11;11). She starts with the most inclusive class and immediately gathers up the whole assortment, proposing as a label the generic term, *Various candles: Because none has the same shape; some have the same shape but they are the smallest and the biggest... and others have different colors and* (and at the same time) *different sizes. So it's not very precise.* When elements are added or suppressed, *anyhow that will be the same as before or even something else.* This leads her to propose a series of possible sub-classes which, when gathered together, are called *various candles* as initially.

To bring unity to such a diversity, some of these subjects start by characterizing the sub-classes by the number of elements, but this reaction is provisional and thereafter they reason as *Fra* does.

SECTION III: TRANSFORMATION OF STRUCTURES
With A. Henriques and D. Maurice

Our next task presents children with objects comprising a structured whole to see whether they are able to reconstitute the same structure with different contents. We have already seen that the seriation structure is so pregnant that it suffices by itself to modify the sizes attributed to the elements, according to their rank in the series. Surprisingly enough, we shall see that children do not always imitate or reconstitute seriation itself when they are given new contents to order, and this is all the more true of more complex structures such as inclusions or intersections. Our materials include the following: 5 nails, identically shaped triangles of various sizes, bangles (with increasing diameters), cards depicting 1, 3, 5, 7 or 9 mice, 10 differently colored rectangles, cylinders with increasing diameters and alternating colors (white, black, etc.). The procedure is to seriate the nails in front of the subject or to present other structured contents and to ask the subject to make similar arrangements with different materials.

5. Seriation

We find three main levels once again. Here are examples from the first level:

INA (4;6). With the five well-seriated nails as a pattern, she thinks her reconstitution is correct when she merely aligns the elements without arranging them in order (1, 5, 4, 2, 3): "Is it the same?" *Yes.* "Are you sure?" *Yes.* "What could you do to get it exactly the same?" (She turns them end down and head up but keeps the same order.) "Could you do the same with the mice?" *Like this* (again, she simply aligns them without taking into account the number of elements.) "And with the bracelets?" (Irregular alignment.)

CAR (4;4). With the same pattern, she produces an irregular alignment of four elements (omitting one): "How did I put them?" (She gives her own order.) "How about this" (same order but in a vertical superposition)? *No.* "And with the bracelets?" (Alignment with errors.) "And with mice?" (She lays out 1, 3, 7, 5.) "Do it again." (Same irregular order.)

YOR (4;6). Pattern: four seriated triangles. Copy: large triangle containing a circle, itself containing a small triangle. Pattern: five seriated nails. Copy: four aligned but unordered triangles.

ERI (4;10). Pattern: five seriated nails. "Choose a collection and do the same." He sets up a large cylinder A, then 4 poorly seriated nails, then a cylinder $B < A$ and a third one $C > B$ and a final large one. The two series are then superposed. (He had mixed them.) "Could you try with the bracelets?" (He nests them.)

FRE (4;6). Pattern: well-seriated yellow mice (1, 3, 5, 7, 9). "Could you do the same with the green triangles?" *No.* "And like this?" (Pattern: seriation of nails.) *Yes.* (He makes a one-to-one correspondence but without any ordination.)

NIC (6;6). Pattern: mice. Reproduction with nails: irregular series. "What did I do?" *In a line.* "What else?" *Straight line.*

Thus, what is kept from the pattern is only its global shape: a linear horizontal succession or sometimes topological envelopments. But the particular relations are ignored or erroneous, especially with respect to the number and the order of elements.

At level II, the advance is in the use of one-to-one correspondences, leading to success in most cases, especially in seriations based on quantities of elements such as the mice. Here are two examples:

SAC (7;0). As with *Fre, Sac* is preoccupied with constructing bijections, and succeeds in reproducing only series with identical numbers of elements: A comparison of four yellow mice with five grey ones won't work *because there are more here.* For five rectangles compared with three cylinders: *No, I can't.*

RIH (7;6). Similarly, despite his successes for equal amounts, he asserts that for five elements facing four, *No, you can't do anything.*

Briefly, although one-to-one correspondence plays a positive role for the subjects, it nevertheless inhibits abstraction of the dominant relation, which is the order that is possible whatever the contents or quantity of materials. On the other hand, subjects do take into account factors such as colors and their alternations, and so forth.

At level III, order at last prevails over the other factors:

DID (7;11) is an intermediate case between levels II and III. After an initial success with five triangles facing five red rings and in a classification of collections according to color, he stumbles over the comparison between 1, 3, 5, 7, 9 yellow mice and 2, 4, 6, 8 grey ones: *They are not the same.* Same problem with 10 rectangles and 5 nails: *It's not the same because there are only five here.* "Is something else the same?" *Yes, that's more and more mice, and there, bigger and bigger nails.*

In the reactions of subjects clearly belonging to level III, we notice an immediate abstraction of order:

VER (7;7) makes six cylinders correspond to eight circles: *I put them according to width* (cylinders) *and to size* (circles). He does likewise with nine nails. Differences in quantity do not prevent the series from *going on with bigger and bigger numbers* (including 4 and 9).

OVE (8;3). *This also goes from the smallest to the biggest*, independently of numbers.

CAL (8;11). *There are more and more here, and there too.*

Even though they always consider it necessary to classify collections according to color, which isn't asked for, these subjects still reproduce the essential feature, which is the ascending order.

6. Boundaries and Intersections

It remains to examine the reconstitution of inclusion and intersection patterns. The task involves either imitating the interviewer's model with new objects, or correctly filling in appropriate contents for Venn diagrams that have been drawn empty. Venn diagrams are taught too early at school, and it is interesting to notice how much they can be misunderstood by younger subjects.

At level I, given a pattern $(x\bar{y}) \lor (\bar{x}y)$, the common part xy has no relation with the other two:

LAU (6;4). In $x\bar{y}$, he puts "the family of daddies" (3 medium red candles) and in $\bar{x}y$ *the family of mommies*, and thus there is no relation between the two classes.

CED (6;4) puts a blue candle in xy, pink candles in $x\bar{y}$, and one white candle in $\bar{x}y$. When he is shown that xy is also part of y, he puts pink candles everywhere.

STE (6;3) gathers medium candles in $x\bar{y}$, round red candles in $\bar{x}y$, and the same in xy as in $\bar{x}y$ (so without having the notion of common parts in xy) *because the "houses" overlap (xy in y):* he doesn't see the reciprocal presence of xy in x.

THA (7;8) puts white candles in $x\bar{y}$, small ones in xy and, in $\bar{x}y$, *the red ones, because it's a color we haven't seen in others,* as if $xy = \bar{x}\bar{y}$ (incompatibility). Whereupon she turns to 3 distinct classes for $x\bar{y}$, $\bar{x}y$ and xy.

LOR at 8 years of age still puts elements in xy which belong neither to x nor to y.

We can see that at this first level the intersection isn't understood at all. *Ced* distributes the objects in three distinct classes, then puts the same objects in all three. *Ste* includes xy in $\bar{x}y$. *Tha* specifically asserts that neither $\bar{x}y$ nor $x\bar{y}$ is in xy, and so forth. In no case is intersection understood as the part which is common to x and y.

At level II we observe an intermediate behavior, in which the intersection xy is filled by adding elements borrowed from $x\bar{y}$ and $\bar{x}y$. This doesn't amount to seeking a common predicate but to adding up two "representatives." Children may also locate in xy elements whose features are intermediate between those of x and those of y:

ANA (7;0) puts straight candles in $x\bar{y}$ and round ones in $\bar{x}y$; in xy are then placed one straight candle and one round one: *One for this family ($x\bar{y}$) and one for that family ($\bar{x}y$)*.

YVE (10;11) puts *the big candles in $x\bar{y}$, the small ones in $\bar{x}y$ and medium ones in xy because they're in between the small ones and the big ones.*

RIC (11;11) gathers the yellow candles in $x\bar{y}$, the red ones in xy and, in $\bar{x}y$, *Orange ones, because (mixing) red and yellow makes orange.*

Finally, at level III the correct solution is either gradually discovered or else found at once:

RIO (7;9). *Straight candles in $x\bar{y}$, round orange candles in $\bar{x}y$ and in xy a long one like those (in $x\bar{y}$), which is orange like the round ones.*

ICO (10;11) puts round red candles in $x\bar{y}$, long white candles in $\bar{x}y$ and one long red candle in xy.

GER (10;7) achieves a correct solution for the intersection of not just two, but three sub-classes.

In spite of what is taught at school, intersection is not understood as quickly as is usually believed, due to shortcomings in the action implications required for the coordination of classes.

7. Inclusions

We use two separate figures to represent inclusion. In the first, which we shall call "sharing," a whole is represented by a circle divided into two parts A and A' by a straight line (or any line); whereas the second one, called "enveloping," uses a large circle or ellipse, the "house," within which is included a small circle, specifically described as one of the "rooms" of the house. The notation for the whole is B, for the small circle A, and for the area surrounding it A': hence, $A + A' = B$. The interesting fact is that understanding inclusion is far easier in the case of sharing than in the case of enveloping, where the subject tends to view A and A' as disjoint classes and not as complementary sub-systems in the same whole B.

Starting with the "houses," here are examples from level I:

CED (6;4) puts a yellow candle in A and two round ones in A'. "And for the whole house" (the word "whole" is stressed)? *These two candles.* (He indicates A.)

ALA (6;6) places one long candle and one round one in A, then puts three of each in A'. "How many are there in the big house" (the whole is pointed out)? *Three round ones and three straight ones* (instead of four): This description characterizes A' and not B.

ANA (7;0). *Round candles in the big garden* (A'), *and straight and wide candles in the small garden* (A). No name is given for the whole.

DIA (7;1). Small pink and white candles in A', small blue and white ones in A, but needs to use two labels and has no name for the whole.

CAR (7;9) has the same initial reactions, but as she doesn't find a name for the whole, she changes the contents of A and puts the same elements as in A'. Hence there is a whole in which, for the child, $B = A'$ and $B = A$.

If we call inclusion a union of sub-classes which have a common predicate on the one hand, and different predicates for each sub-class on the other hand, then there is no inclusion in the reactions observed. The clearest evidence is that, when asked about the number of elements in the whole B (= $A + A'$), the subjects give the number of elements in A' and not in B.

At level II, the whole is characterized by all elements in A and A', through a mere addition and not through a synthesis or a search for a common predicate.

> *DAV* (6;3). Pink candles in A, white ones in A'. "What do you call the *whole* house?" *It's the house of the pink and white candles.*

> *STE* (6;3). Straight medium candles in A, round candles in A', and the whole B is labelled *medium ones and round ones.*

At level III, at last, there is immediate success:

> *TOP* (9;8) puts two straight candles in A', two round ones in A, calling the whole *The set of four candles*—that is, B as such, rather than just A' or a simple enumeration.

> *ENI* (10;11). Round yellow candles in A, round red ones in A' and, for the whole B, *All yellow ones, no* (he laughs), *round ones.*

As for sharing elements in two piles A and A' merely separated by a line, the inclusion of A and A' in a whole B is much easier, since there is no possible confusion between B (= $A + A'$) and the sub-class A'. In the preceding method, the sub-class A' surrounded A, making it all the more difficult to distinguish the whole B from A'. The present task therefore yields correct answers as early as level I:

> *SIM* (5;2) says right away that B is composed of *all the white ones, but these* (A) *are small and those big*: so there is a predicate common to A and A', and two differentiated predicates for A and A'.

> *ANT* (5;5). Brown round ones in A and, in A', a pile of other colors. B is then defined as *a pile of mixed candles.*

> *PAO* (5;7). Round candles in A and, in A', a pile of *long candles with different colors*. B is again *a pile of mixed candles.*

KAR (6;6). *They're all small (B),* but *some of them (A) are standing up and the others are laid down (A').*

NAT (6;11). *The round ones* in *A, the straight ones* in *A'* and *B* is *the pile of 16 candles* (= *A + A').*

When inclusion results from union operations or uniting actions performed by the children themselves, obviously it raises no problem—except, naturally, for the problem we studied earlier of quantifying *A, A',* and *B* when the elements in *A'* are much less numerous than the elements in *A.* This latter case is somewhat similar to our item with nested circles, where inclusion reflects an externally imposed relation.

SECTION IV: SPONTANEOUS ACTIVITIES

We now turn to re-examine the situation with which we began our first studies of this subject: Children's spontaneous activities when provided with heterogeneous objects in complete disorder and when asked to arrange them as they wish and to justify their actions. In fact, such actions end up in classifying objects according to their resemblances and seriating the elements in each collection, which is tantamount to a synthesis of these two operations. However trivial these behaviors may be, we need to understand how they arise out of meanings and action implications, until they are eventually viewed as necessary by the subjects themselves.

At level I, children either construct complex objects by juxtaposing heterogeneous parts to which they subsequently assign meaning, or they assemble disorderly collections that are gathered together step by step without anticipation.

YOL (4;5) takes a large triangle, inserts a small nail in it, then a small circle which itself contains a small triangle. Across one edge of the large triangle she lays a small cylinder, and adds two small rings next to another edge. The whole has no name.

Then she joins side by side a rectangular card and a triangle, adds a new card, then two rings, then a cylinder between the two cards. So this isn't just a cluster, but a chaining which this time receives a name: *It's an elephant in the zoo.* Another chaining of 11 elements is called *a train full of dogs.*

Next, the three cylinders are nested, and the interstices filled with nails. The last shape indicates a tendency towards ordering. Five elements are aligned without being contiguous: two triangles containing cards, then three cards containing triangles. Under this arrangement of five, she hangs five long nails which are then linked to five lower cards that are aligned but not seriated.

NIO (5;5) joins nine variously colored triangles side by side, as in a very uneven but gapless tiling. One of these triangles is called *a dog*, another one *the boat*, and the biggest *a boat*. In other arrangements, nails are joined at their ends, first composing an irregular closed figure with six variously oriented sides, then an arc of a circle, and finally an almost straight series. The nested rings compose the only semi-ordered figure, but still there are two reversals.

LOS (6;6). The final shape is made of six pairs of objects which are tightly clustered side by side, with no overall plan, (2 triangles, 2 rings, 2 sets of nails with their ends pointing to the left or to the right, 2 cards, and at last 2—which is then changed to 3—cylinders).

These elementary reactions bring out an interesting problem of the relation between implications and semi-implications in action. On the one hand, a perceived resemblance between two elements, through an assimilation to the same scheme, implies (in the sense of entailment through a proactive implication) establishing a spatial neighboring relation that is initially purely local, comprising simple pairs. On the other hand, even though it is fortuitous, this neighboring relation entails a shared meaning (see *Yol's* "elephant" and "train"), engendering an elementary structure that is neither a seriation nor a classification, but what we call a "chaining." Therefore, as early as level I, we notice the promise of a structuration, which will be elaborated only as these local semi-implications begin to be coordinated into more systematic implications.

This is what actually happens at level II, when children start classifying elements according to shape and color, but without yet seriating each of the collections:

TIA (6;6) makes classes of yellow cards, green and red triangles, cards depicting mice, and of bracelets, but introduces seriation only with the rings, which he orders from the largest to the smallest with alternating colors.

MAR (6;4). *I've grouped the things that were the same.* "How?" *With color: All the same color* (in each pile). But he seriates only nails: *Ah, in sizes!*

DIA (7;11). Same classifications, with a seriation of the nails. However, in the final arrangement they are no longer seriated, but distributed in two subsets, one ordered and the other in disarray.

SAC (8;3) classifies correctly into subsets, but seriates only a few of them, until she realizes through a sudden insight that the seriation can be generalized: *It's also from the smallest to the biggest*. From then on she orders even the bangles and the cards in numerical order (1, 3, 5, 7, 9), thus attaining level III.

Finally, here are further examples of level III. The first is an intermediate case, in which seriation and classification are combined for all collections except triangles:

NAT (8;1) starts by joining triangles in a shapeless figure resembling the tilings at level I, then he correctly classifies and immediately seriates all the other objects. This done, he is given the triangles again and he once more joins them in a meaningless whole. He seriates the nails, but he also gathers them in a kind of flower, the petals of which are seriated from the smallest to the largest with a fixed starting point.

CHA (7;10), *RIN* (7;7), *SAC* (7;10) and others make small classes according to shape and color, with immediate and correct seriations for each collection without omitting any of the various elements.

Therefore, at level III there is a synthesis of resemblances and differences. This leads us to review the general ideas the chapter has dealt with.

Conclusions

The goal of this somewhat lengthy chapter is to elucidate elementary forms of action implications and their meanings. All of these pertain to establishing resemblance and difference relations in various situations.

With respect to actions that impose relations upon objects, the most elementary and hence the most general implication appears to be a straightforward tautology: "A greater resemblance" implies "a lesser difference" and "a greater difference" implies "a lesser resemblance." This is not at all obvious for young children since, as E. Marti[4] has shown, the relations "more different" and "less similar" are not considered equivalent, and are systematically distinguished, by children aged four or five. In addition, we note that in many situations similarity relations are

---

[4]Marti, E. La négation de la ressemblance chez l'enfant: Différence ou altérité? *Archives de Psychologie*, 1981, 25-45.

translated in terms of spatial neighborhoods and difference relations in terms of spatial separation. In certain cases, neighborhood relations even create or increase resemblance, as with the children in section I who deemed that the middle element M in a seriation changed size when placed near the small or the big element.

The general law that seems to arise from these four sections is that comprehensive classes are initially lacking and instead there is a progressive transition from "paired predicates" and simple chainings to increasingly encompassing and hierarchized classifications. In other words, after an initial period characterized by alternating and local centrations on resemblances or differences, progress in all situations consists in synthesizing both these relations, and this synthesis compels the formation of structured wholes. The simplest of these is seriation, which is an equivalence of the successive differences between each element and its successor. Reciprocally, classifications include a difference between equivalences: Sub-classes of the same rank express an equivalence relation, whereas the hierarchical ordering of classes expresses a difference relation (the less numerous classes being the most encompassing ones, and the more numerous classes being the less encompassing ones). Thus, both seriation and classification require a synthesis of resemblances and differences, and there is a reciprocity between their respective structures. No wonder then that such syntheses develop slowly, and that we find similar difficulties in each of the four sections of the present chapter.

The tools for constructing these syntheses are obviously the action implications that gradually replace the initial paired predicates. For instance: (1) Constructing a class A implies gathering similar items together; (2) but this union implies opposition or differentiations, such as the opposition between A and A'; (3) uniting opposed classes generates a higher ranked class, $(A \cdot A') \rightarrow B$; (4) hence $B \rightarrow (A \vee A')$; (5) seriation implies an iteration of differences having the same magnitude or increasing magnitudes of the same kind; (6) a relation implies conjoined equivalences and differences between n objects; (7) differences imply partial equivalences, since for example, two objects differing in all their predicates are still two objects; (8) resemblances imply that there are various increasing degrees of resemblance before the limit of pure identity is reached.

Such implications are not merely disguised definitions, but actual connections between material or mental actions of the subject. These actions and connections are endowed with meanings, and the relations among these meanings are the implications that arise (along with others, but independent of the causal aspect of action), directly from material actions.

9

CLASSIFICATIONS AND SYMMETRIES

With S. Dionnet, J. Guyon and A. Sinclair

In the preceding chapter, we sought to characterize seriations and classifications in terms of reciprocal relations between similarities and differences. In addition to these two kinds of structures, there is a preoperation that is rather frequent at all ages and which is often combined with the operations of these two groupings, although it is not their source. This preoperation is the construction of symmetries. For any given order of resemblances or differences, to construct a symmetry is to find the corresponding order through a reversal or inversion around a separating axis.

In order to analyze symmetries, we haven't devised situations that demand them. Instead, we use classification tasks to see when and how subjects invoke symmetries that are actually not necessary. The materials are 52 little square cards that differ only in size (two sizes: "big ones" and "little ones") and in color (two colors: pink and blue). Thus, P = big and pink; B = big and blue; p = small and pink; b = small and blue. The experimenter lays down a loose collection of 6 elements (collection I). It takes the form $3P + 3b$ (or $3B + 3p$); $5B + 1p$ (or $5P + 1b$); $5B + 1b$ (or $5p + 1P$); and occasionally $1B + 3p + 2p$. The children are then asked to form another collection with an equal number of elements (collection II) that "go together well," both internally (within II) and between I and II. After this they may proceed to substitutions between I and II, or between both I and II and the pile of remaining elements, with the same instruction to make it "go together well." Two kinds of symmetries can be established: "Internal" symmetries among parts (or sub-collections) of the whole the subject has arranged in II, and "external" ones between collections I and II. Three *B*s opposite three *P*s is an example of the former; an example of the latter is to make $3b + 3p$ in II correspond to $3B + 3P$ in I.

1. Preoperatory Reactions

The problem being merely to construct or to correct collection II and to relate it to the pattern in collection I, we shall distinguish only two developmental levels with respect to what "fits well," both within I and II and in their interrelations, which are mainly brought out by exchanges between them.

NIA (4;11) thinks $3P$ do not fit with $3b$ and should be replaced by $3p$, *because we already have the big ones.* Afterwards he continues matching by color, but for $5B$ and $1p$ in both I and II, he wishes to correct the situation through an exchange: He moves $1p$ from I to II and $1p$ from II to I, without foreseeing that this changes nothing.

VER (4;10) has the same initial reactions, but she substitutes elements of II for elements of I, one by one. "When do we stop?" *When we have exchanged everything,* which changes nothing in the relations between the two collections. Then she proceeds to the reverse exchange, hence recreating her initial collection!

LYM (4;5) likewise exchanges a *B* for another *B* without noticing that neither I nor II is changed.

ITA (5;10). About II, he says that $3B + 3p$ *don't fit well because they are not the same color* and he places $3P + 3p$ in II. As for $3B + 1p$, he reproduces the collection in II, then exchanges the *p* in I for the *p* in II. He holds to the color criterion thereafter, then adds size: $3P + 3p$ *don't fit because they're the same color but this* (3p) *is smaller.*

KAT (5;10). $3P$ and $3b$ go together *well, because they're all the same size.* "How about this one?" *It's smaller but it's another square* (therefore size = shape). "Do they really go together well?" No, because these three (3b) aren't with them. In the case of $3B + 3p$, he produces $3P + 3b$, that is, the inversion of sizes. *You must give me the pink and I'll give you the blue.* He ends up with $5B + 1P$ opposite $5p$

+ 1*b*: *There is still something that doesn't fit.* However, he produces the same two series once again! Then, for 3*P* + 3*b*, he produces the series: 3*B* + 2*b* + 1*p*: "Does that work?" *Yes. You've got three small ones and three big ones and I've got three big ones and three small ones.* Then comes the symmetry: 1*P* + 8*b* for 1*B* + 8*p*, followed by 5*P* + 1*b* for 5*B* + 1*p* and by 4*P* + 3*b* for 4*B* + 3*p*.

SAR (5;6). For 3*P* + 3*b* she first gives 3*B* + 3*p* in II. However, she adds: *We couldn't* (= shouldn't) *put the small ones with the big ones,* and she aligns 3*P* + 3*B* opposite 3*b* + 3*p*. Then she produces 5*P* + 1*p* opposite 5*p* + 1*P* and she spontaneously exchanges the small *p* in I for the big *P* in II. As to 5*B* + 1*P*, she produces 1*b* + 6*p*: *The small ones are there and all the big ones here,* ignoring the colors and the number of elements.

BRI (5;6) gives 3*B* + 3*p* for 3*P* + 3*b*, then 3*B* + 1*P* + 2*B* for 3*P* + 1*B* + 2*P*, reversing the colors and saying, *they fit, they're all big.* However, he inverts 3*P* + 1*p* + 2*P* into 3*p* + 1*P* + 2*p*: He has thus inverted the sizes but accepts an exchange of the middle elements. Similarly for him, 5*B* + 1*p* correspond to 1*P* + 6*p*.

JOV (5;3) produces 1*b* + 5*p* when I is composed of 5*b* + 1*p*, then 5*p* + 1*P* when 5*P* + 1*p* is given.

SER (6;2) gives 1*P* + 5*p* for 5*P* + 1*p*. "Do they fit?" *No, they don't. There are five of them here and one here.* "What can be done?" He places 3*P* + 3*p* on both sides: *Each one has three big ones and three small ones.* So there is a simple correspondence with no inversions. Then he produces 6*b* for 3*P* + 3*B* but says: *This isn't right: There are big Bs and big Ps.* "We can't get it right?" *No, we can't: There are big Ps and big Bs.* He is unable to modify the collections, except for 5*B* in II and 6*b* + 1*B* in I: *This way, it will work: All the small bs with one big one, and only big ones* (P) *here.*

DOZ (6;5). Through a reversal of sizes and colors, he starts with 3*b* + 3*p* opposite 3*P* + 3*B*, then he produces 6*b* opposite 3*P* + 3*B*. "Are they the same?" *Yes.* "Do they go well?" *Yes, they do.* "Why?" (No response.) In order to conform to the heterogeneity in II, he gives 5*P* + 1*b* for 5*p* + 1*P*, then he exchanges one by one up to 6*P* in II and 6*p* in I, but he keeps 1*b* among the *p*s. On the other hand, when he adds elements (as *Sar* and *Ser* also do), *Doz* is not concerned with the number of elements in the collections and may well put 6 or 8 elements in one of them without any numerical correspondence with the 6 elements in the other.

These initial reactions show four striking features. The first is that "to go together well" pertains to just one of the two collections and not the relations between I and II, with the exception of one-to-one correspondences when they are possible through the similarity of elements (for instance, *Ser's* 3P + 3p on both sides). The second is the difficulty of considering simultaneously the two predicates "color" and "size," either because only one of them is involved (such as size with *Sar*), or because subjects forget the first predicate when they turn to the new one. The third feature is that exchanges of elements between collections I and II usually occur only after being suggested by the experimenter. Moreover, they are initially misunderstood to such a point that children don't realize that exchanging identical elements (a p for the same p with *Nic*, a B for a B with *Lym*) has no effect. *Ver* even goes so far as to "exchange everything" one way, then the other way, as if this could change anything. Finally, the fourth noteworthy feature at this level is that when subjects focus on color or size criteria, they often neglect the need for numerical equality between collections I and II: For instance, putting six elements in one collection and seven or eight elements in the other.

2. Operatory Reactions

Here are examples from subjects 7-8 years of age and older (corresponding to the level of concrete operations):

TAN (7;2). "Do your elements go together well?" *You mean with yours?* Thus, he thinks about interrelating the two collections right from the start, when he places 3b + 3P opposite 3P + 3B. *They can be like this* (II) *and like this* (I). "How about the two together?" *Well, no* (but) *we can put the big* Bs *with the small* bs (through exchanges) *then the big* Ps *with the small* ps (colors). "What else?" *Yes, there* (II) *all the small ones and there* (I) *all the big ones.* He does likewise for the rest of the situations.

ANI (7;6) starts, at the outset, with the relations between I and II: *I've got the big blue ones and the small pink ones, and you've got the big pink ones and the small blue ones.* He makes spontaneous exchanges in each situation and says: *Don't give me such easy things to do.* However, in the situation where 5P + 1p is in I and 4P + 1b + 1B is in II, he acknowledges: *Well, they don't fit.* He cannot imagine an exchange that would lead to one single criterion for all elements in each collection.

SEV (8;4) thinks that, in collection I, *they* (3P + 3p) *don't fit well because all of them should be small or all big,* (but) *it works* if they are divided in two subclasses. With (3b + 3p) and (3P + 3B), it is enough to exchange the 3P in II for the

3*b* in I. With 1*B* + 5*b* and 5*P* + 1*p*, exchanges allow modifying the relations between I and II through a classification by sizes.

STO (8;4). For 5*P* + 1*p* opposite 4*p* + 1*b* + 1*P*, no exchange is satisfactory, except when a big element is thought equivalent to two or three small elements.

SCA (8;10). With the same initial reactions, he says that when exchanging the 4*ps* in II for the *P*s in I *it's always the same* (colors), *so they don't fit.*

NIN (10;11). She is the first subject to introduce the number of elements (6 and 6) explicitly in the conditions required for homogenizing collections I and II. In the situation the two preceding subjects faced, she enumerates the various possible exchanges and asserts that none of them is satisfactory. Then she shows what would be acceptable if an element were added in II: *(Then) we could freely make exchanges, (but) this doesn't work, because I have more.* Similarly, in another situation, she suggests adding elements which would permit substitutions, and then she says, *Oh no, we can't because the number* (of elements in I and II) *wouldn't be the same.*

ROB (11;10) enumerates the various substitutions in color and size that would permit comparing collections I and II and he adds, as a third factor, the number of elements: *That would match, because there is the same amount here and there too.*

As compared to the 4- to 6-year-olds, we notice an obvious advance in these reactions. First, the subjects understand at the outset that "going together well" refers not only to the interior of collections I and II, but to their relations as well (see what *Tan* says at the start). Second, they at once and simultaneously take into account the two criteria for resemblance and difference: size and color. Third, by contrast with many 5- to 6-year-olds, they add (first implicitly, then explicitly as *Nin* does) a third criterion, the condition of numerical equality (6 elements in each collection). Fourth, every subject anticipates many possible exchanges (to be brief, we did not enumerate all of them), and they predict the advantages and disadvantages of each. Finally, they divide the collections into sub-collections according to classification rules that have become common at the operatory level.

In a word, in spite of the simple nature of the experiments in this chapter, which seem incapable of establishing a succession of age-related levels, we notice remarkable differences between preoperatory reactions and the behaviors of subjects who have reached the level of concrete operations.

116   TOWARD A LOGIC OF MEANINGS

3. Conclusion: Symmetries

    However commonplace these observations may seem, they show that
before operatory seriations and classifications are formed, a very general
preoperation already intervenes, which is the formation of or search for
symmetries in the broadest sense of the term. Thus, at the first level (4- to
6-year-olds), once the subjects have understood (unlike *Nia, Ver, Lym*, and
Ita) that exchanges or additions modify collections I and II, they construct
several kinds of symmetries. For instance, *Kat* is satisfied with pointing
out that "you have three small ones and three big ones and I have three big
ones and three small ones" (independently of the colors), then with
assembling $1P + 8b$ for $1B + 8p$ and $5P + 1b$ for $5B + 1p$, and so on. *Sar,
Bri* and others have the same reactions. Although these are undoubtedly
forms of symmetries, it is advisable to give this notion a very general
meaning that doesn't require solving a problem with respect to an axis but
only establishing relations of positions.
    To clarify this definition, let us recall the conclusion we have drawn
from the preceding chapter: Seriations consist in similarities between
differences (for instance, between the relations < or >); and classifications
are differences between similarities (for instance, a class A has common
predicates with a class B, in which it is included; the predicates of B are
weaker than in A but are common to all elements in B). These features do
not depend upon positions: The elements in a seriation may well be ranked
in a spatial sequence $a < b < c$, and so forth; nevertheless, these relations are the same if a, b, c are spatially separated and are compared by
means of measurement. In other words, similarities and differences
involved in classifications and seriations are concerned only with contents, irrespective of positions. We may then define symmetry as an
inverse correspondence—a similarity in contents with a reversal of positions.
    With respect to the logic of meanings, these definitions underscore
how its origins go back to the most general coordinations, in which the only
relations are resemblances and differences among contents, on the one
hand, and between contents and positions, on the other hand. In other
words, well before structures themselves are constructed, their internal
connections are prepared by these most elementary relations which will
later become "grouped." Symmetries are interesting in that they seem to
appear earlier than the coordinations preparing the future classifications
and seriations. The reason for this is undoubtedly that symmetries are

made easier by their partially spatial features involving the role of positions. As for the proposed definition of symmetry as an inverse correspondence, of course this doesn't refer to operatory reversibility, but to "revertability."[1]

[1]French = *renversabilité*, a comparison with an original state. This refers to establishing an equivalence through empirical means, independent of any inference that the equivalence is dictated by necessity. (P.M.D.)

CONCLUSIONS[1]

1. The data gathered in this project delineate the elementary onto-genetic forms leading to the construction of operations, and to structures that result from their necessary compositions. Each chapter has shown these developmental roots to be meanings and implications among meanings, starting with action implications that are initially implicit before being consciously grasped and finally being formulated verbally.

As a conclusion, we shall classify the various forms of meanings and meaning implications. To begin with, the simplest are the meanings of predicates. They may be defined as the similarities and differences between one property observed in an object and other predicates that are recorded simultaneously or already known.

Predicates are connected through conjunction-like preoperations which may be either "constrained" (i.e., necessary, hence involving a mutual implication, as in the co-occurrence of shape and size), or "free" (and therefore contingent, as between a shape and a color).[2] In between these two types, we have observed in younger subjects what we have called "coupled predicates" (Chapter 8). These are linked through "pseudo-constrained" conjunctions; for instance, the expectation that the size of the middle element in a seriation can change through a mere change in its position.

It follows that an object is a set of conjoined predicates and its meaning amounts to "what can be done" with it, and is thus an assimilation to an action scheme (whether the action is overt or mental). As for actions themselves, their meaning is defined by "what they lead to" according to the transformation they produce in the object or in the situations to which they are applied. Whether we are dealing with predicates, objects, or actions, their meanings always implicate the subject's activities, which

---

[1]Piaget wrote these conclusions provisionally. (R.G., B.I.)

[2]Wermus, H. Essai de représentation de certaines activités cognitives à l'aide de prédicats avec composantes contextuelles. *Archives de Psychologie*, 1976, *44*, 205-221.

interact either with an external physical reality, or with elements that were previously generated by the subject, such as logico-mathematical entities.

Furthermore, we may distinguish various degrees in meanings: They may remain "local" in that they relate to limited data and to particular contexts; they may become "systemic" in laying the groundwork for structures; and finally they may become "structural" when they pertain to the internal compositions of already constituted structures.

As for the meaning of meanings, it is that they are the only instruments for understanding, in contrast with mere observations which, before being endowed with meanings, can only provide extensions devoid of any intelligibility. The opposition Frege established between *Sinn* (meaning) and *Bedeutung* (denotation) therefore isn't an essential one because the latter is determined by the former. In this regard, the purely extensional truth tables should be replaced by variable extensions that are subordinated to meanings.

2.   Now that we have specified what meanings are, let us recall what they have brought to light about implications. The two problems are indissociably linked: If all truth is based on meanings, and if all forms of meanings consist in attributions of schemes to either predicates, objects, or actions, then clearly there could be no such thing as an isolated scheme or meaning. Rather, there are always multiple relations among them. This means that at all developmental levels, no matter how primitive, all knowledge has an inferential dimension, however implicit and elementary it may be. To put it another way, using a meaning always presupposes and entails using some implications. Let us now review the nature and the various forms of these implications.

In the first place, we have been led to replace the classical extensional implication $p \supset q =_{Def} (p \cdot q) \vee (p \cdot \bar{q}) \vee (\bar{p} \cdot \bar{q})$ where $\bar{p}$ in $\bar{p} \cdot q$ is anything that isn't p (and not just the complementary of p under q) by what we have called the "meaning implication" $A \rightarrow B$, in which at least one meaning of B is embedded in the meaning of A, and this "inherence" relation is transitive (i.e., the meaning of C is embedded in that of B, that of D in that of C, B, A, etc.)

The import of this definition of meaning implication is that, since any action, in addition to its causal aspect (i.e., its being actually carried out), has a meaning, there must be implications between actions, that is to say between their meanings. This is a fundamental reality, going far beyond the realm of implications between statements, and manifested from the beginning of what we have called the logic of actions, which is the necessary basis of operatory logic.

Before discussing the relations between these two logics, let us first notice that action implications, just as implications between statements, may take three forms: (1) a "proactive" form (which Peirce called "predictive"), in which case $A \rightarrow B$ means that B is a new consequence derived from A; (2) a retroactive form (which Peirce called "retrodictive"), according to which B implies A as a preliminary condition; and (3) a justifying form, which relates (1) and (2) through necessary connections that thus attain the status of "reasons." However, we must recall that the reason R_i of a necessary truth can never be isolated. Sooner or later, it brings up the problem of the reason R_j for reason R_i, and so on, through a dialectical spiral that is superimposed on the interconnections between implications of type 1 and 2. This spiral results from the fact that reality draws back to the extent the subject gets nearer to it, because it raises new problems as understanding advances.

3.   These various initial relations, first separately and then through combinations, serve to constitute fragments of structures that progressively become coordinated until "groupings" are formed beginning at about age 7-8 years. The early skeletal structures emerging from interactions among meanings are all the more interesting because they prepare, not only for the formation of concrete operational groupings, but also for the more complex 16 operations found at the formal level, which correspond to the 16 connectives of the truth tables, if these are interpreted in terms of meanings and not in their purely extensional form. Thus, we have witnessed the early establishment of intersections, incompatibilities, and so forth, but at the level of actions rather than of statements. This again demonstrates the general formative role of the logic of actions and action implications in the origination of meaning implications, as opposed to extensional implications.

However, as was pointed out before, if we are to elaborate a logic of meanings, it is advisable to distinguish various forms of the connectives "and" and "or" as well as forms of negations, resulting in a greater number of operations than the 16 operations of extensional logic. The conjunction "and" may be either "free," in which case $p \cdot q$ does not involve a necessary coupling, or "constrained," when $p \cdot q$ becomes $p \leftrightarrow q$. Consequently, there are also two forms of disjunctions and intersections. As for negations, they are always relative to reference frames and are therefore either "proximal" ($A' = B - A$, if B is the reference frame), or "distal" in various degrees.

In the second part of the book, R. Garcia further explicates what we have called operatory logic, which is now founded solely on meanings.

PART TWO[1]
by
Rolando Garcia

[1]This part is from Garcia's original English manuscript.

10

LOGIC AND GENETIC EPISTEMOLOGY

1. Epistemological roots of the Piagetian approach to logic

Piaget is, above anything else, an epistemologist. True enough, he is an epistemologist coming from biology. This does not mean, however, that he is some sort of a "biological epistemologist." Time and time again one reads—or hears—that what Piaget was "really" doing was reducing cognition to a purely biological process, or trying to explain the cognitive system through biology, or even using theoretical biology to explain logic and mathematics.

The whole of Piaget's work on the relations among the sciences has such a strong anti-reductionist flavor that one may wonder how such an interpretation may be seriously maintained.

Although we consider it to be an illegitimate representation of Piagetian epistemological theory, it has, however, some easily detectable roots. We shall mention three assertions of his theory that we consider quite fundamental and that may nevertheless be at the origin of such a distorted interpretation. Genetic epistemology maintains that:

a) There is no point of discontinuity between purely biological processes in a new born child and the very beginning of the child's cognitive processes.

b) Although biological and cognitive systems are *structurally* quite different they both have, *as a common source*, the adaptation of a biological organism to its environment through processes of assimilation and accommodation that perform similar *functions*.[1]

c) The evolution of biological and cognitive systems are both *examples* of the evolution of *open systems* in interaction with their environment. As such, they obey similar developmental *mechanisms*, in spite of all the differences in the characteristics of each domain. Piaget has never formulated this thesis in such terms. It seems, however, that they contain an essential element of his theory.

None of the three assertions involves a denial of the specificity of each field— biological and cognitive—nor do they imply that the "laws" of one field should "explain" the behavior in the other.

Another source of misunderstandings in genetic epistemology, and one that acquires particular significance with reference to this book, is Piaget's permanent concern with logical structures. Once again we want to emphasize that neither the central role of logical structures in Piaget's work, nor his peculiar approach to logic as a discipline, could be clearly understood unless we keep in mind that his concern with logic and mathematics originates in epistemology. His psychological research—the psychogenesis of concept formation—is meant to provide *tools* to understand how knowledge evolves. And biology matters simply because knowledge is something that happens to a particular kind of biological organism and cannot be divorced from it. But the problem of the origin and role[2] of logical structures is a problem that Piaget formulates from an epistemological perspective. It is Piaget the epistemologist, *not* Piaget the biologist, who provides the answers.

2. The epistemological problem of the origin of logic and the role logic plays in epistemology

Piaget's logical theory has two purposes that need to be very carefully distinguished:

[1]See Piaget, e.g., *Adaptation and Intelligence: Organic Selection and Phenocopy.* Chicago: University of Chicago Press, 1980, p. 79. (J.E.)

[2]As a multi-level, cooperative "community" of self-activating action patterns— logic as heuristic and not merely as confirmation (cf. Inhelder, B., & Piaget, J. *The Early Growth of Logic in the Child.* New York: Harper & Row, 1964; e.g., Ch. 6, Minsky, M. *The Society of Mind*; and M. M. Waldrop's piece on Allen Newell, "Soar: A unified theory of cognition?" *Science*, July, 1988, *241*, 296-241). (J.E.)

a) To explain how logical relations and logical structures are developed by the subject (the *knowing* subject!) until they reach the level of what is called the natural logic of a normal adult.

b) To show how logical relations and logical structures play the fundamental role of *assimilatory* instruments that allow the knowing subject to apprehend and organize the objects of knowledge, thus being the necessary conditions for *any* kind of knowledge.

Both processes go together and they interact in accordance with the well known formula: The subject structures the world as he structures his own structuring instruments, i.e., his logic.

The first question (how logic develops) involves in fact one of the most fundamental epistemological problems: Where does logical necessity come from? This has been the Achilles' heel of all theories of knowledge that one finds in the history of philosophy. Plato and Kant gave perhaps the most consistent answers to it—but genetic epistemology was the first to allow this problem to be dealt with in the framework of science and its methods.

Once it was established that logical relations are not innate (nor *a priori*) and that they are neither a *direct* outcome of experience nor obtained from it through the mediation of language (as was claimed by logical empiricism), the task of genetic epistemology was to show how they are constructed by the child. The answer may be simply stated as follows: Logical relations are constructed at the same time that the empirical world is being organized, and they are an inherent part of the organizing processes. But this statement, although not wrong, may be highly misleading. The misleading phrase is "at the same time." This requires some elaboration.

All epistemological theories are, one way or another, attempts to explain how the interaction between the subject S and the object O ($S \Longleftrightarrow O$, for short) generates knowledge.[3] Piagetian theory provides an explanation that involves a truly dialectic interaction process. Let us leave aside, for the moment, what we mean by "explanation" in this context. Saying that knowledge results from a dialectic interaction $S \Longleftrightarrow O$ does not illuminate the problem very much unless we make explicit how the interaction takes place and why we call it a dialectic one. However, it is

[3] For a review, see Piaget, J. Les courants de l'épistémologie scientifique contemporaine. *Logique et Connaissance Scientifique*, Paris: Gallimard, 1967. (J.E.)

easier to start by saying what the statement does not mean. It clearly does not mean any sort of "action and reaction" process, as some oversimplified versions of dialectic materialism may suggest. It does not mean a Hegelian "affirmation-negation-overcoming" process either. Generation of knowledge by a $S \Longleftrightarrow O$ process is not like a spark between hydrogen and oxygen producing water. It is a laborious and complex process having specific "moments" (or periods) that cannot be mixed together.

This is all familiar Piagetian theory. There is, however, one point that —as simple as it is—is often overlooked. When the subject S faces a given situation, in his interaction with O he *reads* the situation (the empirical data) by using the organizational (logical) instruments *already* constructed in *previously* experienced situations. Through such instruments, empirical data become *observables*, i.e., they are interpreted (which means that they are somehow organized). In turn, the new situations the subject S is facing (and thereby *interpreting*) will help in building *new* assimilation instruments, i.e., organizers and logics, by means of which he can interpret *other* situations.

We ought, perhaps, to apologize for reminding the reader of these elementary ingredients of Piagetian theory, but we need them to bring up what seems to us a basic misunderstanding one finds in the comments of some very competent logicians criticizing Piaget's logic. They refer to what they call "the myth of stages" in Piaget's developmental logic as a singling out of *some* periods that Piaget considers of overall importance in the development of logical relations, whereas "in fact" he should have distinguished many more "steps" of at least equal significance. We would submit that those logicians, when making such a criticism, are acting *just* as logicians. They overlook the fact that whenever Piaget makes distinctions among stages he does it from an *epistemological* viewpoint. Let us pause for a moment to spell out what this means.

3.   Piagetian stages and the self-organization of open systems

One of the fundamental tenets of genetic epistemology is the assertion that the development of the cognitive system is *neither a continuous growth nor a linear process*. The existence of stages is just an expression for these two facts. In this, Piaget in psychology (perhaps together with Freud) and Marx in political economy have pioneered what nowadays is called a general systems theory. We know today that open systems, i.e., systems that exchange matter, energy, information, etc. with the environment, are self-organizing systems. This means that such systems acquire an internal structure that becomes stabilized when the exchange fluxes representing the interactions with the environment become stable.[4]

The key word in this formulation is "stability." That a structure is stable by no means implies that it is static. It does not imply either that it is under equilibrium conditions, in the sense given to this word in classical thermodynamics. A structure may be stable (1) because it is under equilibrium conditions, or (2) because, *being far from equilibrium conditions, it is kept in near steady state conditions through exchanges with the environment.*[5] In the first case the word "equilibrium" may be applied without qualifications. In the second case it may not be. We may talk then about *dynamic equilibrium*, or we may coin another word, as Piaget did, calling it *equilibration*.

In the case of a cognitive system, as in any manifestation of a living organism, we are far from equilibrium conditions. If we cut off the exchanges with the environment, the organism evolves towards equilibrium. And in this case, equilibrium is death. When the exchanges with the environment go on, the biological organism and the cognitive system are kept far from equilibrium conditions.

We have learned from the results of genetic psychology, as interpreted by genetic epistemology, that the cognitive system can be viewed as an open system whose dynamics are determined to a large extent by exchanges with the environment. Such a system evolves through periods of dynamic equilibrium or "near steady state conditions" (the stages), followed by disruptions in the equilibrium (disequilibration) and re-organizations (re-equilibration) that put the system in new steady state conditions. Actually, we must make a distinction between "steady state conditions" and truly "stable" conditions. That conditions *far from equilibrium* remain steady means that the system fluctuates around some mean. These

[4]Nicolis, G., & Prigogine, I. *Self Organization in Nonequilibrium Systems.* New York: Wiley, 1977, p. 41. See also Prigogine & Stengers, *Order Out of Chaos*, Toronto: Bantam, 1984; and Prigogine, *From Being to Becoming*, New York: Freeman, 1980. (J.E.)

[5]An equilibrium condition is usually defined in physics as meaning that small pertubations of the system are reversed by the system itself so that it returns to the original condition, e.g., a pendulum hanging free. A pendulum in a clock, however, as long as it receives energy from its environment, can maintain a steady state—beating time. (J.E.)

fluctuations are due either to *internal* variations, or to *external* variations in the environment. Beyond a given threshold, the fluctuations generate an instability in the system: This is the disruption point in the steady state conditions (disequilibration).

The stages in Piagetian developmental theory of knowledge are: periods of relative stability (*not* in equilibrium, *not* static!) with all sorts of fluctuations that arise from the changing situations with which the subject is being confronted. The transition from one cognitive stage to the next is a typical case of an unstable system that cannot assimilate certain perturbations any more (internal contradictions, inability to solve a given type of problem, etc.) and must reorganize the assimilatory tools for new situations.

Each period—each stage—is characterized by the sorts of problems the subject is capable of solving (what sort of situations he is able to cope with). This is clearly an epistemological characterization of stages, not a logical one. Logical considerations come afterwards: solving problems, coping with situations, explaining what is happening under such and such conditions, require the use of logical relations. In each period—in each stage—the subject makes use of certain characteristic logical relations. Not one, but many. Not *a* logical structure, but *many* of them. Each one of them has its own (very complex) development. These developmental lines do not coincide. It follows that *the developmental stages are not established by the development of single logical relations as such.* (Which one should we so privilege?)

To say that there are characteristic structures in action at each stage is very different from saying that the stage is *defined* by *a* logical structure. Piaget's formulation of stages involves the first assertion, not the second. Let us see, very schematically, how the stages are characterized. We shall consider only the levels of conceptualization, leaving aside the sensorimoror period.

4. Cognitive stages and logico-mathematical links

One may distinguish three important steps in the evolution of logico-arithmetic links. These steps correspond to the three classical stages described in genetic psychology and designated with the names of "pre-operatory thought," "concrete operations" and "hypothetical-deductive reasoning." More recently, in connection with the study of the common mechanisms between psychogenesis and the history of science, such steps were characterized by three kinds of logico-arithmetic links which have been called "intra-operatory," "inter-operatory," and "trans-operatory."[6] We believe that these denominations represent the actual meaning of the stages more clearly than the former ones. This was agreed upon by Piaget. He wrote himself in our book: ". . . these three stages. . . correspond to the succession 'intra', 'inter' and 'trans'. This is what we shall show through examples before dealing with the reasons that make such a progression a necessary one and that justify identifying three stages (as in the "theses," "antitheses," and "syntheses" of classical dialectics) instead of a distribution into any other number."[7]

4.1 Intra-operatory links

The intra-operatory links are those that refer only to internal articulations. The lack of reversibility at the intra-operatory level implies that the relations remain isolated and are not combined into transformational systems nor (even less) into structures. There are two main classes of such links, with little or no coordination between them:

a) *Comparisons and correspondences*, which are formed in the step preceding the constitution of functions. Within this class we find identities (not in any way a simple kind of relation) as well as those correspondences that result from repetitions, similarities and equivalences. Functions also belong here, but only insofar as they do not imply transformations and their invariants.

b) *Transforming actions*, which are of various kinds, such as:

- collections of objects that are divided in sub-collections (e.g., the familiar division of a class B into subclasses A and A', yet without any understanding of the quantification attached to the inclusion relation),
- seriation of objects of various different sizes A, B, C,... (only when it comes out of empirical verifications which do not involve transitivity),
- natural numbers (but without any conservation of quantity).

---

[6]Piaget, J., & Garcia, R. *Psychogenesis and the History of Science.* New York: Columbia University Press, 1989.

[7]*Ibid.*, p. 174.

4.2   Inter-operatory links

The *inter-operatory links* are those that involve *elementary opera-tions*, such as forming sets, seriations, etc., with compositions among operations, leading to the first rational logico-arithmetic structures. At this level we find coordinations among correspondences and among transfor-mations, as well as conservation principles. The following relations are established:

- reversibility
- recursivity
- transitivity
- commutability[8] (and its linear form: commutativity)
- limited associativity
- reciprocity

What needs to be explained is the transition from intra- to inter-operational links. This requires, in particular, an explanation of how the child goes from being the "putting-together" coordinator and the coordi-nator of succession, to (using) the operations which appear in the later period. In this transition, Piagetian theory now assigns the central role to the conquest of *commutability*, although the elaboration of this idea came rather late within the theory[9]: The understanding that the modifications that take place at the "point of arrival" are related to the modifications that took place at the "point of departure" is in fact the most fundamental step in the transition to this period. This has two important consequences: a) direct transformations are coordinated with inverse transformations thus leading to the *operations* that go far beyond one directional actions; and b) the child may thus conceive of *conservations*.

In addition, the possibility of retroaction and retrospection will lead to recursivities, transitivities and reciprocities.

The central problem of this stage comes, then, from the fact that the characteristic structures which may be built—the groupings—although being already quite consistent and having a high degree of generality, are still very "poor" and present important limitations. Recall that the group-

---

[8]Cf. Piaget, J. *The Equilibration of Cognitive Structures*, Chicago: The University of Chicago Press, 1985, pp. 96-97. (J.E.)

[9]Inhelder, B., Blanchet, A., Sinclair, A., & Piaget, J. Relations entre les conserva-tions d'ensembles d'éléments discrets et celles de quantités continues. *Année Psychologique*, 1975, 75, 23-60.

ings are the characteristic structures of this stage (and in fact they constitute the only effective structural organization in the qualitative logic of this period), but they *do not* provide *the* definition of the stage.

We should not dwell here on the well known limitations of the grouping. It seems, however, worthwhile to make reference to the *epistemological* problems thereby implied: why there are such limitations, and how they are overcome.

The first limitation refers to the way this structure performs its function. In fact it expresses qualitative properties of certain exogenous contents. As such, the grouping is always *subordinated* to contents that are given, i.e., extra-logical. This explains why they are very weak structures from the formal point of view, although they have a consistency which enables them to be formalized.[10] Moreover, the subordination to an extralogical content explains why this structure has such a degree of generality at the psychogenetic level, which may cover a long period between 7 and 11 years of age, during which the subject begins the work of logically coordinating its operations but without being able to go beyond the organization of concrete contents (due to the lack of formal, hypothetico-deductive mechanisms).

A second limitation which is characteristic of the groupings is the fact that there is no composition except between neighboring elements (or subsets). At this level, there is a quantification but it is restricted to "all," "some" or "none." To be able to combine any two elements (or subsets) requires extensional generalizations not yet developed by the child. On the other hand, in so far as compositions are subordinated to extra-logical materials, there is no possibility of relating *forms* as such, and therefore the subject is confined to those connections that are related to the contents.

A third limitation systematically found in the groupings has to do with the difficulties related to conceiving class intersections which lead chil-

---

[10]Groupings have been identified as categories, in the sense of Saunders MacLane, which suggests a richer heuristic potential for their development than does Garcia's logically accurate critique. For reviews, see Easley, J. A., Jr. Mathematical foundations of forty years of research on conservation in Geneva. *Focus on Learning Problems in Mathematics*, 1979, *1*(4), 7-24; and Davidson, P. M. Piaget's category-theoretic interpretation of cognitive development: A neglected contribution. *Human Development*, 1988, *31*, 225-244. For a full development see Piaget, J. *Morphisms and Categories: To Compare and Transform*. Hillsdale, NJ: Lawrence Erlbaum Associates (in press). (J.E.)

dren to consider only disjoint classes and thereby, in the case of classifications, to proceed by dichotomies.

Finally, the limitation that perhaps summarizes all of them is the
impossibility of deducing the properties of a subsystem starting with the
properties of the total system. This is the essential reason to consider the
grouping as a weak structure.

4.3   *Trans-operatory links*

Trans-operatory links are those leading to logico-mathematic structures of a clear algebraic nature such as groups, combinations, proportions,
etc. At the level corresponding to children 11 to 12 years old they appear
spontaneously but they do not go beyond an instrumental use. They are not
"thematized," and they characterize only a "know-how" of the subject,
which does not yet involve understanding the structures as such. However,
under this simple form of utilization without any reflective objectivation,
those structures result from a very constructive process that applies
operations on operations. This is clear in the following cases:

a)   *Permutations*, which require the establishment of an order among
the various different possible seriations because the set of permutations is
obtained as a seriation of all seriations.

b)   *Combinations*, which are classifications of all classifications.
The novelty introduced at this level is that the child does not operate only
with disjoint classes but rather with classes having an increasing number
of intersections.

c)   *The set of subsets*, which comes out of the preceding structure by
adding a new factor, i.e., vicariance (or substitution-Ed.). The passage
from one *vicariance* to another involves in fact going from one system of
inclusions to another, together with the multiple partitions and intersections thereby implied.

The set of all subsets of a given set results from a generalization of this
process.

d)   *The INRC group*, which includes both inversions and reciprocities.

This kind of group appears (only *instrumentally* and not yet thematized) each time that two different systems are composed into a single
totality. Such is the case, for instance, when a single motion is referred to
two different reference frames (in relative motion) with the necessary

coordination among them.[11] The two-valued propositional logic is *also* an example of such a group.

The transition from "inter" to "trans"

> shows that, once an operation is formed, and even though it is as close to common actions as an ordering, it doesn't remain long in an inert and isolated state ('intra') but sooner or later constitutes a structural kernel which expands indefinitely in the directions 'inter' and 'trans' until it reaches the construction of structures proper.[12]

5. Diachrony, synchrony and logical structures

The expression to be emphasized in the above quotation is "structural kernel." The developmental lines of all structurations converging into—and diverging from—this "kernel" do not coincide. This, once again, shows that the idea that Piagetian stages are defined by the development of logical relations taken in isolation from one another is untenable.

Two other points need to be taken into account to put Piagetian stages in their proper perspective. Let us quote again from the same text:

> Such cognitive hierarchies include two kinds of nestings. Some are proactive through the broadening of all domains in the successive periods of the construction of knowledge. Others are retroactive because what is acquired at level n can enrich relations which have been formed at the previous level $n - 1$.[13]

This leads to the second point we want to stress:

> This being so, it seems that we may conclude that the series Ia, Ir, T (i.e. "intra", "inter" and "trans") does not consist of simple and therefore linear overtakings, as in any elementary dialectical succession; on the contrary, there is a continual overtaking of the very tools for overtaking, which gives cognitive tools their specific fecundity and complexity.[14]

[11]Cf. Inhelder. B., & Piaget, J. *The Growth of Logical Thinking*, New York: Basic Books, 1955; and Easley, J. A., Jr. Comments on the INRC group. *Journal of Research in Science Teaching*, 1964, 233-235. (J.E.)
[12]Piaget and Garcia, *op.cit.*, p. 180.
[13]*Ibid.*, p. 183.
[14]*Ibid.*

Here we find the core of the problem we are discussing: Each stage cannot be conceived as simply a natural *growth* of the preceding one; each stage *re-organizes the whole of the instruments already used by the subject.* In that view, how can one possibly think of this transition in terms of a growth and, as Apostel suggested,[15] look for a growth algorithm, to represent the actual development of children's conceptual frameworks? It is rather surprising to find how persistent this idea is, in spite of the fact that Piaget has clarified this point (in our view, in a very conclusive manner) quite a few years ago. Thus, for instance, in his comments on Apostel's paper in Volume 15 of the *Etudes d'Epistémologie Génétique*, Piaget takes exception to the idea of "deducing *a priori* what such a development must be from its most humble beginning to its 'final' state by means of an essentially algebraic structural analysis."[16] The outcome of such an approach was clearly judged by Piaget: "It could possibly lead to some generalizations that would be interesting from a formal viewpoint, but that might have no genetic significance."[17]

We beg to apologize to the reader for dwelling a bit more on the significance of this assertion.

The temporal process of painfully constructing a system of relations should hardly be thought of as being exactly parallel to a rational reconstruction of the strictly formal links among the components of the system. In fact, the situation is as follows. Let us consider a stage n and its transition to a stage $n + 1$. Both n and $n + 1$ are characterized by the *instrumental use* of logical structures that we shall call S_n and S_{n+1}, respectively. We have then *two different* problems: a) how the system of relations S_n generates, operationally, i.e., in action, the system S_{n+1}; b) how the system S_n that is subsumed in the system S_{n+1} is formally inserted in S_{n+1}. The answer to the first problem requires a *diachronic* study (an empirical one) of how the mind of a subject is evolving. The answer to the second problem requires a *synchronic* study of the *formal* relationships among various structures. The first problem is the task of the epistemology of logic. The second problem is the task of logic.

[15]Apostel, L. The future of Piagetian logic. *Revue Internationale de Philosophie*, 1982, 142-143.

[16]Piaget, J. Introduction: Le problème de la filiation des structures. In L. Apostel, J.B. Grize, S. Papert, & J. Piaget. *La filiation des structures.* **Etudes d'Epistémologie Génétique**, Vol. 15. Paris: Presses Universitaires de France, 1963, p. 10.

[17]*Ibid.*, p. 11.

No wonder that logical analysis finds that "in fact" there is a larger number of steps to go from the formal S_n to the formal S_{n+1} than the developmental epistemologist would claim! This simply means that the child's or the adolescent's mind does not follow the rigorous paths of the formal logicians. But it does not need to. Children grasp a structure (in action) and operate with it, ignoring the formal logician's warnings. In this, children are not different from scientists. "Pure" mathematicians seriously objected to P.A.M. Dirac's delta functions. Fortunately Dirac did not bother with that and went on using them in his version of quantum mechanics. When L. Schwartz provided an adequate foundation for such functions, his rigorous way of constructing them was quite different from Dirac's.

The reciprocal is also true. We know very well that the logician cannot formalize everything that a knowing subject does in his "logical thinking." The well known limitations of formalisms are now commonplace, but it may not be superfluous to remind ourselves that even the simple operation of making one-to-one correspondences between sets cannot be completely formalized when infinity is involved. This well known consequence of the Löwenheim-Skolem theorem[18] is just one among the many arguments to show that intuition cannot be completely formalized. It is true that there are other possible interpretations of this theorem which avoid any such consequences, but this is always at the expense of "drastic solutions" requiring a high price to be paid concerning the resulting theory of mathematics.[19] In fact even in such cases the problem is not solved, but just shifted to other areas.

The idea of trying to find too close a parallelism between "the filiation of structures" from the psychogenetic viewpoint and the internal, synchronic, static interrelations among logical structures of an increasing degree of complexity, takes form in Apostel and others' project to find "a structural order relation among algebras which would partially or completely reflect the genetic relation of a filiation among systems whose

---

[18]See for instance the masterful analysis by John Myhill: On the ontological significance of the Löwenheim-Skolem theorem. Reprinted in I. M. Copi & J. A. Gould, *Contemporary Readings in Logical Theory*. New York: The Macmillan Company, 1967.

[19]See the interesting analyses made by Hao Wang in his paper: On denumerable bases of formal systems. In Th. Skolem, et al. *Mathematical Interpretation of Formal Systems*. Amsterdam: North Holland, 1955.

operational forms would be represented by such algebras."[20] We have already referred to the answer given by Piaget to such a proposal: the multiplicity of possible developmental lines that may be found through such a purely theoretical analysis is very great; only a judicious combination of psychogenetic empirical work and epistemological analysis will provide the answer about which one of those possible ways of development actually takes place (children and adolescents are very stubborn in this respect). But this is only a partial answer, involving only one of the problems presented by the attempts to construct a "genetic algebra." The second answer, already mentioned, is connected with the limitations of formalisms. We shall not dwell on this here.

There is, however, a third answer that is, in our opinion, much more fundamental from an epistemological viewpoint. The main objection to a "genetic algebra" comes from the theory of cognitive development which, as we pointed out above, is closely linked to the theory of the self-organization of open systems. Let us pause for a moment to spell this out.

6. Structural discontinuity and functional continuity

The diachronic and synchronic aspects of the development of the cognitive system are related in a specific way. Such an evolution has been described above as a succession of stages, i.e., a succession of near steady state conditions undergoing equilibrium disruptions. Each one of these stages typically uses "assimilatory tools" that define the kind of problems that the subject can solve and the kind of "explanations" that he will propose for certain situations.

In the case of cognitive growth in the child, the assimilatory tools are primarily logical relations. The transition from one stage to the next will not be depicted as some sort of "addition" of new elements to the existing ones. Each transition means a complete *re-organization* of the previous "stage." This, in turn, means that the former dynamic equilibrium has been destroyed. The theory of transition from one stage to the next is, above all, a theory of the disruption of equilibrium states. The parallel to this in physical theory is the instability of an equilibrium state. Once the *instability* is triggered off, the system is *disorganized*, and, under certain conditions, it may find new patterns of organization. We shall come back to this

---

[20]Apostel, L. Structure et genèse. In L. Apostel, J. B. Grize, S. Papert, & J. Piaget, *op. cit.*, pp. 67-68.

point (which is much more than a mere analogy). As far as the cognitive system is concerned, "disequilibration" represents a process where the subject is unable to cope with certain problems by using the assimilation structures he has been able to build up until now, and the whole system enters into a crisis.

When we say the "whole system" we refer of course to the *structural* aspects of the cognitive system, *not* to the *functional* aspects. The instruments and mechanisms for constructing knowledge continue to be in action. It is precisely through their application that the subject will be able to *re-organize* his system. This re-organization means a clear cut *discontinuity* in the transition from one level to the next. But the discontinuity is structural, not functional. Cognitive development is thus characterized by structural discontinuity[21] and functional continuity.

Within the theory of genetic epistemology, the re-organization process is conceived of as taking place through the utilization of some specific *cognitive instruments*. The central role is played here by what Piaget has called "reflective abstraction." The very way in which it enters the process of constructing new structural relations prevents any idea of a continuous line of development or growth. One may question the validity of such a building process as depicting the actual cognitive development. But the questioning has to be stated in psychogenetic and epistemological terms, *not on logical grounds*. Once again, it is Piaget's epistemology that is involved. No amount of formal logical arguments may settle the problem.

This being so, the way we understand today the evolution of open systems under varying environmental conditions provides a further and stronger argument in the same direction. In fact, when a physical (open) system becomes unstable, its ulterior evolution is essentially unpredictable. The point representing the unstable state on the path of the system is in fact a branch-point, and there is more than one possible path that the system may follow. This inherent unpredictability of the exact path followed by a system which goes through successive periods of instability (disequilibration) seems to be a characteristic of all open systems. The theory of stages in cognitive development is quite consistent with such an assertion.

---

[21]The structural discontinuities from one level to the next form the obstacle that stands in the way, as already indicated above, of any attempt to construct a "growth algorithm." (Not in the original French edition.) (J.E.)

We need to come back to a point that we left pending. Logical operations are not built in isolation, nor are they constructed all at once. As it will become clear from reading the present book, logical relations are slowly being built up as fragments of structure which are gradually coordinated among themselves until some new structures with more coherent internal organization emerge. Such is the case with the "groupings," for instance. A child does not acquire a command of groupings just by classifying objects or by putting them in a certain order. All this needs a preparation consisting of the elaboration of various kinds of logical links, some of which are already isomorphic with respect to the connectives of propositional logic, but still far from being coordinated in a single system. The way such coordinations take place represents a very complex process not yet studied in full detail. At a given moment, there is a convergence of various structural fragments in what we referred to above as "a structural kernel." And, as already pointed out, each "fragment" may find itself at a different "level of development" from the others. The stage is therefore not defined by any of those single lines of development but rather by what the child is able to do with all the fragments of structures he has built so far. The complexity of the process at the psychogenetic level is such that little hope is left for a genetic "algebra."

11

EXTENSIONAL LOGIC AND INTENSIONAL LOGIC

1. Arguments supporting extensionality

Formal logic, in the tradition starting from *Principia Mathematica* (even if it was preceded by G. Frege and in a certain sense by C. S. Peirce and E. Schröder[1]) has been, by and large, extensional logic. For almost half a century this version of logic, with a number of variations, dominated the field. All of us who were involved in the teaching of courses in "modern logic" back in the middle of the century could show the students that in spite of the efforts made by traditional philosophers to keep Aristotelian logic alive, the latter was unable to account for the logical reasoning required by quite elementary mathematics. This part of the battle was easy to win because we could give clear cut examples showing the extreme limitations of "traditional" (Aristotelian) logic.

---

[1]Frege cites E. Schröder's *Lehrbuch der Arithmetik und Algebra*, Leipzig, 1873. See p. xx and passim in G. Frege, *The Foundations of Arithmetic* (trans. J. L. Austin, second revised edition), New York: Harper & Bros., 1960. (J.E.)

The second part of the battle—the introduction of truth-functional logic—was not exempted from difficulties. It was nice to show the students how to use truth tables stressing the fact that the "tables" for the logical connectives of "conjunction" and "disjunction" were what we "really mean" when we say "and" and we say "or." The problems started with "implications" ($\supset$). We experienced the same difficulties that we sensed in our own teachers of logic when we were students. How to get around the so-called paradoxes of "material implication"?

The truth-functional value of $q \supset p$ is true, if p is true, even if q is false and has "nothing to do" with p. So we had to admit *and to teach* that the statement, "If all Swiss are Moslems, then the French are Europeans," is an "acceptable" statement and, in addition, that it is a true statement. Of course no one speaks that way—not even an "extensional logician" when he speaks to his wife.

We soon learned how to convince the students that although the results obtained by a truth functional definition of "$\supset$" in fact looked a bit strange, there was nothing to be worried about. We did it in several steps. First we avoided the word "implication" to get away from the usual connotations, and replaced it by "conditional." Then, we divorced the conditional "$\supset$" from the common reading "if ... then ...." Then we even avoided using any truth table to introduce the "$\supset$," and said that "$p \supset q$" was simply an abbreviation for $\overline{p \cdot \overline{q}}$, so we could keep only the more comfortable truth tables for "$\cdot$" and "$-$." Then we admonished: Don't ever take "$\supset$" and the ordinary "if ... then ..." as synonyms; a true scientist does not need the "if ... then ..." to carry on his work. One of the foremost logicians of our time, W.V.O. Quine, expressed all this with admirable clarity:

To begin with let us picture formal logic as one phase of the activity of a hypothetical individual who is also physicist, mathematician, *et al.* Now this overdrawn individual is interested in ordinary language, let us suppose, only as a means of getting on with physics, mathematics, and the rest of science; and he is happy to depart from ordinary language whenever he finds a more convenient device of extraordinary language which is equally adequate to his need of the moment in formulating and developing his physics, mathematics, or the like. He drops "if-then" in favor of "$\supset$" without ever entertaining the mistaken idea that they are synonymous; he makes the change only because he finds that the purposes for which he had been *needing* "if-then," in connection with his particular scientific work, happen to be satisfactorily manageable also by a somewhat different use of "$\supset$" and other devices. He makes this and other shifts with a view to streamlining his scientific work, maximizing his algorithmic facility, and maximizing his understanding of what he is doing. He does not care how inadequate his logical notation is as a reflection of the vernacular, as long as it can be made to serve all the particular needs for which he, in his scientific program, would have otherwise to depend on that part of the vernacular. He does not even need to paraphrase the vernacular into his logical notation, for he has learned to think directly in his logical notation, or even (which is the beauty of the thing) to let it think for him.[2]

Teachers of logic, 30 years ago, were very reassured by the words of Quine. However, those of us coming from the empirical sciences did not feel so much at home with what he said. Only a "pure" logician (or, for that matter, a "pure" mathematician) could "let the logical notation think for him." No real physics would ever come out of such "thinking." This uncomfortable feeling did not go beyond that, but other difficulties added to it, namely that some of the consequences of using the truth functional definition of "$\supset$" *did not* agree with the actual construction of scientific theories. The most serious case is provided by the truth functional validity of the formula $p \cdot \bar{p} \supset q$ which indicates that by asserting a contradiction, the logic becomes trivial, i.e., one may assert *any* statement whatsoever.

This result is not only a "strange result." It is untenable. It is not true that in physics, for instance, if a theory involves a contradiction then any assertion whatsoever may be asserted within the theory. Of course, a "pure" formal logician may answer: "But you are using the expression 'if … then …,' and you had agreed to divorce '$\supset$' from 'if-then' so your conclusion is not right." However, Quine speaks of "physicists, mathematicians, *et al*" [sic!] as only having need of "$\supset$" to make their own science. What sense could we attach then to the *validity* of "$p \cdot \bar{p} \supset q$ for any q"?

Anderson and Belnap, in connection with this 'anomaly,' refer to a remark made by S. C. Kleene to the effect that, in the first version of Quine's *Mathematical Logic*, B. Rosser was able to deduce Burali-Forti's

[2]Quine, W. V. O. Mr. Strawson on Logical Theory, *Mind*, 1953, *63*.

paradox,[3] but *not* Cantor's paradox.[4] This simply means that both Rosser and Kleene accept the fact that a logical theory involving a contradiction (Burali-Forti's) does not imply *any* statement (Cantor's paradox, for instance). And here we are not in any sort of "impure" physical theory. This is *pure* logical theory at its best.

Considerations of this kind have led some logicians to question the adequacy of truth functional logic for the theoretical scientist. Efforts to reintroduce "intensions" in logic started in the late fifties and gradually developed into a clear-cut alternative logical theory. The most comprehensive presentation of such developments that took place in roughly the twenty years following Ackermann's paper, *Begründung einer strengen Implikation* (1956),[5] is found in Anderson and Belnap's book.[6]

2. The logic of relevance and necessity

We shall try to present an extremely short summary—and, as such, it will be very incomplete and not quite accurate—of some of the basic ideas

[3]Bunch, B. H., in his *Mathematical Fallacies and Paradoxes*, (New York: Van Nostrand Reinhold, 1982), writes, "The Burali-Forti paradox is sufficiently unpleasant that when it was shown to appear in a system of logic devised by W. V. O. Quine, he felt forced to make major changes in the system.

"The Burali-Forti paradox arises from the fact that you can build a new ordinal number from each preceding one. This series of ordinal numbers also has an ordinal number. That ordinal number ought to be somewhere in the series. But like the set T in the proof that the number of subsets is greater than the number of members of a set, this ordinal can be shown not to be in the series of ordinal numbers. This is a contradiction, but in this case, unlike the proof, there is no assumption to contradict—unless the whole theory is abandoned." (pp. 129-130). (J.E.)

[4]Bunch (*ibid,* p. 130) summarizes Cantor's paradox as follows: "Cantor had shown that for any set whatsoever, the set of subsets of the set contains more members than the set itself. What about the set of all sets?

"Since the set of all sets includes all possible sets, each of its subsets must be members of it. So there cannot be more subsets than there are members of the set of all sets." (J. E.)

[5]Ackermann, W. Begründung einer Strengen Implikation. *Journal of Symbolic Logic*, 1956, *21*, 113-128.

[6]Anderson, A. R., & Belnap, N. D. *Entailment: The Logic of Relevance and Necessity.* Princeton and London: Princeton University Press, 1975.

of what that book proposed as a "logic of relevance and necessity." We do that in order to show the *convergence* between such a proposal and Piaget's approach to logic. We stress the word "convergence," because we do *not* maintain that the logic of relevance, in any of the possible varieties presented by Anderson and Belnap, is in any way a formalization of Piagetian logic. We don't even know, as we pointed out in chapter 10, what meaning could be attached to the expression "formalization of Piagetian logic." This notwithstanding, the convergence between the logic of relevance (LR, for short) and the operatory logic (LO, for short) does not seem to us to be a mere coincidence in the way of approaching certain key problems concerning the structure of logical theory. We would go a little further than that.

The convergence between LR and LO takes place on three fundamental points:[7]

a) Logic starts from inferences, and inferences are primarily implications between meanings.

b) Logical connectives in propositional logic are introduced *via* inferences (i.e., implications).

c) Truth-functional logic is just one special case among a large variety of possible links among propositions, some of which are more adequate than others to depict the kind of relations among statements in scientific reasoning.

Let us start with LR. Anderson and Belnap joined the group of logicians who wanted to restore the "if-then" with full rights back into logical theory. They want to have a logical system where "implication" and "conditional" mean something very close to what they mean in ordinary language (granting that ordinary language is far from being consistent and precise). To that effect they introduce a concept of "entailment" for the notions of logical implication "expressed in such logical locutions as 'if ... then ...,' 'implies,' 'entails,' etc., and answering to such conclusions—signalling logical phrases such as 'therefore,' 'it follows that,' 'hence,' 'consequently,' and the like." The sign '→' is adopted, and '$A \rightarrow B$' is interpreted to mean 'A entails B.'[8]

---

[7]This paragraph with its three points does not appear in the 1987 French edition. (J.E.)

[8]*Ibid.*, p. 5.

In order to fulfill the intended objective, two conditions are required to assert that $A{\rightarrow}B$: relevance and necessity. A "pure calculus $E_{\rightarrow}$ of entailment" is presented that "does capture the concepts of necessity and relevance in certain mathematically definite senses."[9]

The requirement that the implication '$A{\rightarrow}B$' be "necessary" goes beyond the notion of "validity" used in truth-functional logic. We may say that "necessity" refers here to a "necessary validity." A necessary implication requires therefore that A and B have "something in common"—they cannot be entirely independent of each other as in the case of the so-called material implication. It is required that B be relevant with reference to A.

It is important to point out that "relevance" may be defined independently of "necessity," while a definition of "necessary implication" which does not involve relevance is not acceptable in the intended formalization of "natural implication." It is therefore clear that whenever we refer to a necessary relation of the kind '$\rightarrow$,' we are referring to a "necessity *cum* relevance."

The idea of attaching the requirement of "necessity" to a relation of the kind '$\rightarrow$' was already advanced in 1932 by Lewis and led to the development of modal logics. To fulfill his purpose Lewis applied a one-place operator "$\Box$" to a truth-functional relation. Thus, "$A{\rightarrow}B$" (intended to mean that A necessarily implies B) was interpreted as "$\Box F(A, B)$" where $F(A, B)$ is a truth-functional relation between A and B. However, an operator like "$\Box$" *cannot* capture the requirement of *relevance* between A and B.[10]

Leaving aside modal operators, LR has taken another road to arrive at an entailment solution preserving necessity *cum* relevance. The way that has been chosen consists in defining '$\rightarrow$' on the basis of a system of acceptable inferences. The starting point will thus be a system of *natural deduction*, and inference becomes the central node of logic.

Anderson and Belnap have shown—in a convincing way—that Gentzen's system of natural deduction, with slight modifications, is a system that: (a) is "acceptable," in the sense that it adequately represents that kind of reasoning actually used in scientific work (whatever this may

---

[9]*Ibid.*, p. 6.

[10]c.f. the section: "Relevance is not reducible to modality," by R. K. Meyer, in Anderson and Belnap, *op.cit.* § 29.12, pp. 462-471.

mean in more "precise" terms), and (b) allows the building up of a formal system, providing the means to define "natural implication" as well as all other logical connections having the required characteristic of being both relevant and necessary.

The proposed construction amounts to asserting that $A \rightarrow B$ if and only if there is a possible way of taking us *deductively* from A to B. "Entailment" in this sense becomes thus the converse of deducibility.[11]

The method is based on a rule of "Entailment Introduction" ($\rightarrow I$) to the effect that we can assert $A \rightarrow B$ whenever there exists a deduction of B from A, or, in other terms, a proof of B from the hypothesis A. The proof should be a scheme such as:

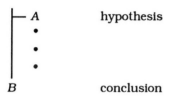

A	hypothesis
$\bullet$	
$\bullet$	
$\bullet$	
B	conclusion

where we have to fill in the dots in accordance with very strict rules. In fact, a system of natural deduction is defined by the set of rules that allows us to fill the gap represented by the dots.

An example of such a system is the one called **FH$_\rightarrow$** by Anderson and Belnap with the following five rules:[12]
1. *Entailment Introduction* ($\rightarrow I$): If a scheme like the above is a valid deduction of B from A, then $A \rightarrow B$ follows from that deduction.
2. *Entailment Elimination* ($\rightarrow E$): Whenever $A \rightarrow B$ is asserted, we shall be entitled to infer B from A.
3. *Hypothesis*: In the course of a deduction beginning with a supposition A, we may begin a new deduction, as a subproof, with a new hypothesis B.

---

[11]i.e., $A \rightarrow B$ if and only if B is deducible from A. (J.E.)
[12]*Ibid.*, pp. 7-9.

4. *Repetition*: We may repeat ourselves within an outer proof or within a subproof.[13]

5. *Reiteration*: A step following from A in the outer proof (as indicated in rule 3) may also be repeated under the assumption B in the subproof.

The following is an example of a proof of the law of transitivity of entailment (additional vertical lines are used to set off the two subproofs):[14]

1	$A \rightarrow B$	Hypothesis
2	$B \rightarrow C$	Hypothesis
3	$A \rightarrow B$	1 Reiteration
4	A	Hypothesis
5	$A \rightarrow B$	3 Reiteration
6	B	4, 5 $\rightarrow E$
7	$B \rightarrow C$	2 Reiteration
8	C	6, 7 $\rightarrow E$
9	$A \rightarrow C$	4, 8 $\rightarrow I$
10	$(B \rightarrow C) \rightarrow (A \rightarrow C)$	2, 9 $\rightarrow I$
11	$(A \rightarrow B) \rightarrow [(B \rightarrow C) \rightarrow (A \rightarrow C)]$	1, 10 $\rightarrow I$[15]

Although the above proof is satisfactory, the system as such is not, because as it stands it allows for "proofs" where the final implications asserted do not meet the requirement of being *both* necessary *and* relevant. Therefore, in addition to imposing restrictive conditions on the reiteration rule, a technique is needed that would allow an A to be introduced only when A is relevant to B in the sense that A *is used in arriving at B*. The technique is based on using sets of numerals as subscripts for the formulas. There may be as many nested subproofs as needed, but each must have a

---

[13]Rule 4 seems to have been inadvertently omitted from the 1987 French edition and the English manuscript. The paragraph begins in both cases by mentioning five rules but lists only four, and rule 4 is also found as rule 2 among the revised rules listed below. The wording of rule 4 above follows Anderson and Belnap closely (*op.cit.*, p. 7). (J.E.)

[14]*Ibid.*, p. 9.

[15]A, B, C, here, are sentential variables, not the numerical or object variables, predicates, or constants, that one ordinarily sees represented by capital letters in Piaget's writing. So transitivity of entailment between sentences A, B, and C should not be confused with transitivity of relations between objects, usually written $A > B > C$ or $C < B < A$. (J.E.)

distinct numeral for its hypothesis, and the steps should follow the track of those numerals. The resulting system $FE_\rightarrow$ presents the above rules revised in the following way:[16]

1. Hyp: A step may be introduced as the hypothesis of a new subproof, and each new hypothesis receives a numerical singleton set $\{k\}$ as a subscript, where the numeral k is also new.
2. Rep: A_a may be repeated, retaining the relevance indices a.
3. Reit: $(A{\rightarrow}B)_a$ may be reiterated, retaining a.
4. $\rightarrow E$: From A_a and $(A{\rightarrow}B)_b$ to infer $B_{a\cup b}$.[17]
5. $\rightarrow I$: From a proof of B_a on hypothesis $A_{\{k\}}$ to infer $(A{\rightarrow}B)_{a-\{k\}}$, provided k is in a.[18]

The application of these rules is rather cumbersome, but it is proved that such a system of natural deduction (called $FE_\rightarrow$ by the authors) is equivalent to a pure calculus of entailment ($E_\rightarrow$) based on the following laws:[19]

$E_\rightarrow$:	1.	$A{\rightarrow}A$	(identity)
$E_\rightarrow$:	2.	$(A{\rightarrow}B){\rightarrow}[(B{\rightarrow}C){\rightarrow}(A{\rightarrow}C)]$	(transitivity)
$E_\rightarrow$:	3.	$(A{\rightarrow}B){\rightarrow}[A{\rightarrow}(B{\rightarrow}C){\rightarrow}C]$	(restricted assertion)
$E_\rightarrow$:	4.	$[A{\rightarrow}(B{\rightarrow}C)]{\rightarrow}[(A{\rightarrow}B){\rightarrow}(A{\rightarrow}C)]$	(self distribution)

Once this fragment of logic has been built, the construction of LR proceeds by steps. First, negation is added to entailment ($E_\rightarrow$) showing that a calculus of entailment and negation can be developed independently of other truth functional connectives. Second, the other connectives are included by considering "first degree entailments," i.e., formulas $A{\rightarrow}B$ where A and B can be truth functions of any degree not containing

---

[16]*Ibid.*, p. 23.

[17]$\rightarrow E$ (Entailment Elimination) requires that the conclusion's subscript $\{1,2\}$ show that B derives relevantly from A and from $(A{\rightarrow}B)$. Thus, from $(C{\rightarrow}A)_{\{1\}}$ and $(A{\rightarrow}B)_{\{2\}}$ we can infer $(C{\rightarrow}B)_{\{1,2\}}$. (*Ibid.*, p. 7.) (J.E.)

[18]$\rightarrow I$ (Entailment Introduction) subtracts an element, e.g., it subtracts $\{1\}$ from the two-element set $\{1,2\}$, indicating that a hypothetically introduced antecedent has been incorporated and discharged. Thus, from the conclusion of the footnote above, incorporating hypothesis $\{1\}$, we could infer $[(C{\rightarrow}A){\rightarrow}(C{\rightarrow}B)]_{\{2\}}$. The subscript, by identifying the undischarged hypothesis $A{\rightarrow}B$, which is still assumed, blocks irrelevances that truth functions, $FH_\rightarrow$ and other formal deducibility systems allow, e.g., from hypothesis B and axiom $A{\rightarrow}A$, to infer $B{\rightarrow}(A{\rightarrow}A)$. (*Ibid.*, p. 18.) (J.E.)

[19]*Ibid.*, p. 24.

entailments. Finally, all fragments of the system are combined together in a single calculus of entailment ($\mathbf{E}_\rightarrow$) preserving the requirements of necessity and relevance and thereby avoiding the paradoxes of extensional logic.

The second step mentioned above is of particular interest for us. The authors call "tautological entailments" those first degree entailments that are valid. The main concern here is to take into account the relevance of antecedent to consequent when both are purely truth functional. The way to do it is by referring to the *content* of both antecedent and consequent. Let us see very briefly how this is carried out.

We consider a finite set of propositional variables $p, q, r, \ldots$. The following definitions are then introduced.

ATOM: A propositional variable or its negation (i.e., $p, \overline{q}, \overline{r}, \ldots$)

PRIMITIVE CONJUNCTION: An expression like $A_1 \cdot A_2 \cdot \ldots \cdot A_m$, where each A_i is an atom.

PRIMITIVE DISJUNCTION: An expression like $B_1 \vee B_2 \vee \ldots \vee B_n$, where each B_j is an atom.

PRIMITIVE ENTAILMENT: An entailment $A \rightarrow B$ where A is a primitive conjunction and B is a primitive disjunction.

ENTAILMENT IN NORMAL FORM: An entailment $A \rightarrow B$ having the form $A_1 \vee \ldots \vee A_m \rightarrow B_1 \cdot \ldots \cdot B_n$, where each A_i is a primitive conjunction, and each B_j a primitive disjunction.

EXPLICIT, TAUTOLOGICAL PRIMITIVE ENTAILMENT: A primitive entailment $A \rightarrow B$ such that some (conjoined) atom of A is identical with some (disjoined) atom of B.

EXPLICIT, TAUTOLOGICAL ENTAILMENT IN NORMAL FORM: An entailment $A_1 \vee \ldots \vee A_m \rightarrow B_1 \cdot \ldots \cdot B_n$ where, for every A_i and B_j, $A_i \rightarrow B_j$ is explicitly tautological.

Entailments in normal form are taken to be valid if and only if they are explicitly tautological. The procedure to determine validity of first degree entailments is to convert them into normal forms. Then the validity is established by application of the following rules.

RULE I: $A \rightarrow B$, where A and B are atoms, is valid if and only if A and B are the *same* atom.

RULE II: $A \rightarrow B$, where A is a primitive conjunction and B a primitive disjunction is valid if and only if some atom A_i of A coincides with some atom B_j of B.

Example: $p \cdot q \rightarrow q \lor r$ is valid

$\bar{p} \rightarrow q \lor p \lor r$ is *not* valid

$p \cdot \bar{p} \rightarrow q$ is *not* valid

RULE III: An entailment $A \rightarrow B$ is valid if there is a normal form $A_1 \lor \ldots \lor A_m \rightarrow B_1 \cdot \ldots \cdot B_n$ such that for each couple A_i and B_j the entailment $A_i \rightarrow B_j$ is valid in accordance with rule II.

Example: $p \cdot \bar{p} \cdot q \rightarrow p \cdot q$ is valid

$(\bar{p} \lor q) \cdot (\bar{q} \lor r) \rightarrow (\bar{p} \lor r)$ is not valid, because the normal form $(\bar{p} \cdot \bar{q}) \lor (\bar{p} \cdot r) \lor (\bar{q} \cdot q) \lor (q \cdot r) \rightarrow (\bar{p} \lor r)$ is *not* valid since $q \cdot \bar{q} \rightarrow \bar{p} \lor r$ is not valid.

Let us see somewhat more in detail how the above rules are applied.

a)   EXAMPLES OF VALID ENTAILMENTS

(i) $(p \cdot q) \lor \bar{p} \rightarrow (\bar{p} \lor p) \cdot (\bar{p} \lor q)$ is valid because the following entailments are valid

$$p \cdot q \rightarrow \bar{p} \lor p$$
$$p \cdot q \rightarrow \bar{p} \lor q$$
$$\bar{p} \rightarrow \bar{p} \lor p$$
$$\bar{p} \rightarrow \bar{p} \lor q$$

(ii) $p \cdot q \rightarrow q \cdot (r \lor p)$ is valid, because the following entailments are valid

$$p \cdot q \rightarrow q$$
$$p \cdot q \rightarrow r \lor p$$

b)   EXAMPLES OF ENTAILMENTS THAT ARE NOT VALID

(i) $(p \cdot \bar{p}) \lor q \rightarrow q$ is not valid because $q \rightarrow q$ is valid but $p \cdot \bar{p} \rightarrow q$ is not valid

(ii) $p \rightarrow p \cdot (q \lor \bar{q})$ is not valid because $p \rightarrow p$ is valid but $p \rightarrow q \lor \bar{q}$ is not valid

It is important to point out that the above rules lead to the result that all valid entailments are tautologies whereas not all tautologies of the truth-functional (extensional) calculus are valid entailments. The following example is very instructive in this respect.

$$\bar{p \cdot q} \rightarrow (\bar{p} \cdot q) \lor (p \cdot \bar{q}) \lor (\bar{p} \cdot \bar{q})$$

is *not* valid in spite of the fact that it represents the truth table of "$\lor$" applied to the case $\bar{p} \lor \bar{q}$ (which is equivalent to $\overline{p \cdot q}$). In order to show this, it is enough to reduce the above expression to its normal form and to verify that each atom of the antecedent $\bar{p} \lor \bar{q}$ does not entail each one of the conjunctive terms of the consequence.

This notwithstanding, the following entailment *is* valid.

$$(\bar{p \cdot q}) \cdot (p * q) \rightarrow (\bar{p} \cdot q) \lor (p \cdot \bar{q}) \lor (\bar{p} \cdot \bar{q})$$

where p*q is the complete affirmation:

$$p*q=_{df} (p \cdot q) \vee (\overline{p} \cdot q) \vee (p \cdot \overline{q}) \vee (\overline{p} \cdot \overline{q})$$

Tautological entailments of the kind described above (first degree entailment) may be formalized as follows:[20]

ENTAILMENT:

Rule: from $A \rightarrow B$ and $B \rightarrow C$ to infer $A \rightarrow C$

CONJUNCTION:

Axioms: $A \cdot B \rightarrow A$
                  $A \cdot B \rightarrow B$

Rule: from $A \rightarrow B$ and $A \rightarrow C$ to infer $A \rightarrow B \cdot C$

DISJUNCTION:

Axioms: $A \rightarrow A \vee B$
                  $B \rightarrow A \vee B$

Rule: from $A \rightarrow C$ and $B \rightarrow C$ to infer $A \vee B \rightarrow C$

DISTRIBUTION:

Axioms: $A \cdot (B \vee C) \rightarrow (A \cdot B) \vee C$

NEGATION:

Axioms: $A \rightarrow \overline{\overline{A}}$
                  $\overline{\overline{A}} \rightarrow A$

Rule: from $A \rightarrow B$ to infer $\overline{B} \rightarrow \overline{A}$

This formalization of tautological entailments is just a fragment of a full calculus of entailments. It has the interesting features of using truth-functional connectives but through an intentional implication relation that avoids the known fallacies of purely extensional logics.

A system including the various fragments referred to above may be built in various ways. Anderson and Belnap propose one system E with 14 postulates and only two rules:[21]

$\rightarrow E$:   given $A \rightarrow B$, from A to infer B
\&I: from A and B to infer $A \& B$ (where the sign '&' stands for
              the conjunction represented as '·' above).

The fact that both rules are needed is explained by the authors in the following way:

---

[20]*Ibid.*, p. 158.
[21]*Ibid.*, p. 232.

The system E is designed to encompass two branches of formal logic which are (as we have been arguing in the course of this entire treatment) radically distinct. The first of these, historically, is concerned with questions of relevance and necessity in entailments, both of which are at the root of the logical studies from the earliest times. The second, extensional logic, is a more recent development to which attention was devoted partly in consequence (we believe) of the fact that the first was more recalcitrant—purely extensional logic *can* be developed in a mathematically interesting way simply by ignoring the problems of relevance and necessity, which got logic off the ground in the first place. Since E covers both kinds of territory, it is not surprising that two kinds of primitive rules are needed: the first, $\rightarrow E$, having to do with connections between truth values, where relevance is not an issue.[22]

In addition to combining features of both intensional and extensional logic, this way of building up a logical formalism presents the advantage of allowing for the introduction of other kinds of connectives having some of the properties of the known truth-functional connectives, but not all of them. Intensional connectives therefore find a natural place in logical systems having the same rights to "legitimacy" as the current text-book formal systems of extensional logic. Let us consider one of such alternatives.

It is well known that the so-called disjunctive syllogism expressed by the truth functional relation

$$A \cdot (\bar{A} \vee B) \rightarrow B$$

presents serious difficulties if taken to represent the way a scientist (let alone an "ordinary" person) carries out his reasoning. In particular the acceptance of the disjunctive syllogism would have the unwanted consequence

$$A \cdot \bar{A} \rightarrow B$$

for any B, which we have rejected as not representing the logical structure of scientific theories. The difficulties disappear, however, if instead of using an extensional '$\vee$' that may relate propositions A and B which are completely independent of each other, we define an alternative "or," to be represented by '$\underline{\vee}$,' in such a way that

$$[A \cdot (\bar{A} \underline{\vee} B)] \rightarrow B$$

---

has the meaning of
$$[A \cdot (A \to B)] \to B$$
where '$\to$' is the (intensional) entailment. This means that '$\underline{\vee}$' becomes defined as
$$A \underline{\vee} B =_{Df} \bar{A} \to B$$
If, on the other hand, we accept De Morgan's law between conjunction and disjunction, the above definitions of '$\underline{\vee}$' would have, as a counterpart, an analogous intensional conjunction (to be represented by 'o') given by:[23]
$$A \text{ o } B =_{Df} \overline{\bar{A} \underline{\vee} \bar{B}} = A \to \bar{\bar{B}}$$
Such a connective has already been referred to in the literature by Lewis, Goodman, and others. Anderson and Belnap adopted the name of "cotenability" for this sort of connective. It is clear that it has some properties of the extensional conjunction: commutation, associativity, and transitivity. It *does not* have, however, some others. In particular

$A \text{ o } B \to A$ is *not* valid.

We shall come back to this in the next section.

Our sketch of some fragments of an LR was only intended to introduce basic elements of a fruitful method for constructing logical systems. Such a methodology is a purely formal one. Its authors present it as collections of rules that are either *ad hoc* tools for reaching certain goals, or working hypotheses which help to see "where we get to" with any given rule. This highly flexible approach to logic is a valuable tool for the "genetic epistemologist" who is looking for the roots of "natural logic" in an adult who is not affected by the theory.

3.   **The relationship between the logic of relevant and necessary implications and the logic of meaning implications**

We have already, in the preceding section, referred to a certain "convergence" between the logic of entailment (LE) and operatory logic. With reference to the latter, we have to distinguish between what is written in the *Essai de logique opératoire* (LO)[24] and a renewal of it on the basis of a logic of meaning.

---

[23]Since, by analogy with $\overline{p \cdot q} =_{Df} \bar{p} \vee \bar{q}$, De Morgan's Law, $\overline{A \text{ o } B} =_{Df} \bar{A} \underline{\vee} \bar{B} = A \to \bar{B}$, from the definition of $\underline{\vee}$ above. (J.E.)

[24]Piaget, J. *Essai de logique opératoire.* Paris: Dunod, 1972 (Second Edition, revision by J. B. Grize, of Piaget's *Traité de logique*, 1949).

This "renewal" should consist primarily in a rewriting of that part of LO that refers to propositional logic, by incorporating a logic of meaning on the basis of the material presented in this book. This is obviously a work still to be done, but we believe that the road to be followed is clear. We shall refer to this new version, that would come out of the fusion of LO and the logic of meaning, as LO'.

The convergence between LE and LO (and, *a fortiori*, LO') finds its origin in the way the logical theory is built up. Logic, in the tradition of *Principia Mathematica* (PM), was born in a period when Bertrand Russell's logical atomism dominated his philosophy. In turn such a philosophical position was an expression of the dominating paradigm in the physical sciences by the end of the nineteenth century. No wonder that the "building blocks" of logical theory were taken to be elementary propositions and their combinations by means of simple "connectives." No wonder either that the elementary propositions were called "atomic" and their combinations were called "molecular." Starting in this way, the PM logic had to look for its own foundations in purely linguistic considerations. Logical empiricism was quite consistent, in this regard, and spelled out what was the natural epistemological implication of such a way of approaching logic, by making explicit its own philosophy of logic: In fact, logical connectives, according to this school, expressed nothing but the internal structure of our language. This epistemological viewpoint carried with it another implication that is the one of interest for us in the present context: The propositional logic springing out of such positions had to be extensional. Extensionality was thus not an arbitrary decision of the builders of modern logic. It was the natural choice to which they were led by their epistemological position.

The first similarity we find between LE and LO' is that both react against this presentation of logic. The reasons are, however, quite different. In LO', the building up of logic is guided by epistemological considerations, whereas in the case of LE the construction is purely formal. In spite of this difference, both take *inference* as the starting *process* to build up a logic.

From the point of view of genetic *epistemology*, logic starts at the moment a child is able to anticipate a relation between actions (when and how this happens are questions to be answered by genetic *psychology*). Anticipation of actions means *inference*. Piaget's dictum—"at all levels, even the most elementary ones, any form of knowledge includes an inferential aspect, however implicit or elementary it may be"—is an essential founding block of his epistemological theory. Let us insist—and this cannot be overemphasized in view of what we said in chapter 10— that this is an *epistemological* assertion based on the *empirical* findings of genetic *psychology*.

It was therefore clear that, from the developmental point of view, logic starts long before propositions, that logical relations are not based on linguistic relations, and that the propositional calculus could not claim to be necessarily the first chapter of a book of logic.

Inference already involves a logical relation: *implication*. As it is shown in this book, implications are first found at the level of actions (in fact, a relation between actions is an implication). Implications between statements come much later. In both cases, however, they are meaning implications, in the sense explained in the various chapters of this book. "Pure" extensionality is here excluded at the outset.

LE proceeds in a similar way but for different reasons. Here the leading idea is to get away from extensionality in order to avoid its disturbing consequences: paradoxes of material implication, difficulties with the disjunctive syllogism, etc. Starting with inferences and defining (acceptable) implications, i.e., entailments, on the basis of inferences, was in fact the way out. But this is done on strictly formal bases, by establishing very precise rules. They look a bit artificial, but this is just what they are: *ad hoc* rules to reach the intended objectives.

We shall come back to this point, but need first to make two remarks. In the first place, by introducing the entailment relation in LE, on the basis of "acceptable" inferences, the variety of logical connectives that may be introduced afterwards, corresponding to a large variety of possible entailments between statements, is greatly enlarged. This diversification of connectives is quite in line with what is found at the psychogenetic level, and becomes an essential feature of LO'.

A second and no less important remark is that by the above procedure, extensional connectives find their proper place and may be introduced without carrying with them the known paradoxes of the traditional propositional calculus.

These features of both LE and LO' were in fact already present in the *Essai de logique opératoire* (LO). This may seem to be a wrong assertion to those who open Piaget's *Essai* and find that propositional calculus is presented extensionally and that the structure of the calculus is arrived at by analyzing truth functions and truth values. This is due to the fact that LO contains a strange mixture of elements, some of them belonging to extensional logic and others not. In this respect, we dare to say that this part of LO, in the way it is written, does not follow naturally from the former chapters. Moreover, we believe that such a presentation of propositional logic was a concession made to current presentations of logic in the Whitehead-Russell traditions, and that Piaget never was at ease with such a solution.

We remember an expression used by Piaget at the beginning of the year—at the International Center for Genetic Epistemology—when the studies reported in the present book were going to be started: "We must clean up my logic." This is just a proof of the assertion we made above. The "mixture" of elements in Piaget's treatment of propositional calculus in LO shows that he used extensional logic with great precautions. It is a fact that he introduced extensional definitions of logical connectives and that, in particular, he defined the implication relation through its truth table. This notwithstanding, his *interpretation* of propositional logic, based on the inclusion relation among classes, is free from the paradoxes of material implication. Moreover, it may also be taken as an interpretation of entailment in the sense of LE.

In this context, the convergence between LE and LO (and—*a fortiori*—LO') is not purely coincidental. The interpretation of LO that we have just mentioned provides a clear meaning to the "rules" of the logic of entailment that in the presentation of LE appear as being only some *ad hoc* interdictions adopted in order to achieve certain pre-established results. This is not immediately obvious in LO, but it is now made more explicit in LO'.

In fact, the rules for an "acceptable" entailment already mentioned in the preceding section, are just expressing the kind of relationship described by Piaget as "the nesting of a part in a whole, or of a part in itself." In the case of Rule I (p. 150), the correspondence is trivial since it only expresses the nesting of a class with itself.

Concerning Rule II, it is enough to simply take the typical example that has the form

$$P \cdot Q \rightarrow R \vee Q$$

Its interpretation in terms of classes would be

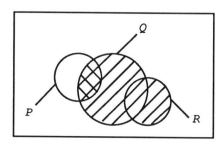

which corresponds to the nesting of $P \cap Q$ in $Q \cup R$.

Rule III is just an extension of Rule II and it could be reduced to successive applications of the latter.

With the above interpretation, the rules of entailment cease to be *ad hoc* rules and acquire a clear meaning.

A problem arises when other connectives are introduced *through* entailments and when one attempts to analyze the structure of the resulting propositional calculus. It is clear that there are many possible axiomatic systems that could be built on the basis of the intensional implication. Anderson and Belnap describe and analyze quite a few of them which have been proposed in the last 25 years. They made a systematic study of these axiomatic systems, showing their inter-connections and the kind of calculus we arrive at.

We have already mentioned two consequences that are of great importance for LO'. First, entailment, i.e., *intensional* implication, does not exclude a calculus with extensional interpretations of "not" and "and." Second, there are many possible versions of an intensional calculus.

With reference to the second remark, the question arises as to the criteria for deciding that a certain connective is "indeed" a "conjunction" or a "disjunction." The connective "co-tenability" ("o") referred to in the preceding section is not accepted by Anderson and Belnap as being a conjunction, because from $A \circ B$ we cannot infer A. We believe, however, that "o" could be considered as the only legitimate way of expressing a *conjunction* of A and B when they belong to a system where the *parts* cannot be asserted independently of the *totality* they belong to. In this respect, the psychogenetic studies leading to the kind of formulation of logic characteristic of LO' become very useful. They show the complexity of situations out of which some logical relations will emerge that would admit a certain degree of formalization.

Finally, it should be stressed, once more, that what is now needed is an explicit formulation of LO'.

12

GENERAL CONCLUSIONS

The purpose of this book was to describe some elementary forms of children's responses to simple problems, in order to show the psychogenetic roots of logical relations, leading to operations and their compositions in structures.

The central thesis put forward by Piaget is that, even at the most elementary levels, knowledge always involves some inferential dimension. The problem was to find out what this inferential dimension consists of. The answer may be stated very briefly: at the most elementary levels, inferences are just implications between meanings (which are attributed to properties, to objects, and to the actions themselves). This requires some clarification based on some fundamental tenets of developmental psychology.

1.   Meanings result from an attribution of assimilation schemes to objects, the properties of which are not "pure" observables but always involve an *interpretation* of the "data." In accordance with the classic definition of schemes ("a scheme is what can be repeated and generalized in an action"), we shall say that the meaning of an object is "what can be done" with the object, and this definition applies not only to the sensorimotor level but to the pre-operatory level starting with the semiotic function. However, meanings are also what can be said of objects, i.e., descriptions, as well as what can be thought of them, when classifying or relating them and so on.

As for actions themselves, their meaning is "what they lead to" according to the transformations they produce in the objects or situations on which they bear. Whether predicates, objects, or actions are involved, meanings imply that the subject's activities interact either with an external, physical reality, or with a reality the subject himself has previously generated, as in the case of logico-mathematical entities.

2.   Elementary actions as well as higher order actions could not exist nor function without links relating them. Thus schemes of actions are never isolated. There are various kinds of links among schemes and thereby various meanings resulting from their applications. The most general kind of a link is a relation of implication.

It is essential in this respect to establish a clear distinction between two different aspects of the relations among actions: the causal relationships, and the implicative relations. The former are centered on the objects and they are concerned with the results observed once the actions have been performed. The latter are relations between meanings and as such they are susceptible of being anticipated.

There is in fact a progression or transition from material actions and their coordinations (the meanings of which are only partially brought out once the movements have been performed), to coordinations of actions whose results may be anticipated. In the latter case the meanings prevail at the very level of anticipations. In other words, any meaning supposes and entails the use of some implications that do not come down to implications between statements and that intervene in the early transition from actions coordination to inferential compositions. We have here the beginning of logic. Even though an action is neither true nor false, and is only assessed in terms of its efficiency or usefulness with respect to a goal, the action implications involved in anticipations may be true or false and therefore constitutes a logic from the most primitive levels on.

We may now reformulate what we called above the central thesis of this book: There is a logic of meanings preceding the formal logic of statements; such a logic of meanings is based on implications between meanings or, what amounts to the same thing, implications between actions.

3.   The most characteristic feature of the logical links elaborated by the children already at the level of actions, but later on among statements, is that these elaborations take place *on the basis of meaning implications.* Whether they are implicit or explicit, these implications may theoretically (*i.e., from the observer's standpoint*) be reduced to combinations of

implications and negations. In other words, at all levels, the foundation of any logic is inferential, which is natural in the case of a logic of meanings.

In chapter 3 the empirical results that have been obtained show the evolution of three kinds of inferences characterizing three quite distinctive levels:

a) Anticipations which are limited to what is allowed by observable repetitions of arrangements or modifications which have already been empirically observed. At this level, the subject reasons or infers only about a domain of empirical objects.

b) Inferences in anticipations which go beyond what is observable and are based on implications which, even though they are necessary, do not yet provide their own "reasons." They are action implications which, instead of being confined to drawing the logical consequences of empirical abstractions, are based on a "reflective" kind of abstraction.

c) Inferences based on "reasons" or on possible demonstrations.

On the other hand, meaning implications undergo a very characteristic evolution. In chapter 7 a distinction was made between forms or *degrees* of such implications, found at three different levels:

a) *"Local" implications*: In this case the meaning of actions is determined by the observed outcomes. Implications are data- and context-bound.

b) *"Systemic" implications*: Implications are inserted in a system of relations which are established through step-by-step understanding. At this level the first judgments on possibility and impossibility appear (see the weaving in chapter 7). These inferences, however, do not suffice to reach necessary "reasons." Necessity and generality are still undifferentiated.

c) *"Structural" implications*: They bear on the internal compositions of previously constituted structures. There is, at this level, an endogenous understanding of the "reason" for the observed general facts. The *general* relationships in level (b) now become *necessary* ones.

4. Meaning implications are threefold in another way. Such action implications may take the following forms:

a) *Proactive implications*: They draw conclusions from the propositions involved; that is, they assert that if $A \rightarrow B$, the Bs are new consequences derived from A.

    b)   *Retroactive implications*:[1] Instead of dealing with consequences, they relate to preliminary conditions and they express the fact that if $A \rightarrow B$, then A is a preliminary condition for B.

    c)   *Justifying implications*: This form of implications relates forms (a) and (b) through necessary connections reaching the "reasons."

In other words, implications have a threefold orientation—*Amplification* bears on consequences; *conditioning* bears on preliminary conditions; and *deepening* brings out the reasons.

    5.   Once the semiotic function is elaborated, action implications go with statements, hence the formation of meaning implications between statements. Once again implications are determined by meanings and cannot be reduced to extensions. Consequently, we can and we must construct a logic of meanings whose central operation will be the "meaning implication." In such a logic, the symbol "$\rightarrow$" will designate this implication. We shall write $A \rightarrow B$ if a meaning M of A is included in the meanings of B and if this shared meaning M is *transitive*. In that case, intensional meaning embodiments ("inherences") correspond to extensional nestings, and therefore to truth values. However, the latter are partial and are determined by meanings, and there is a relativization of negations according to their nestings as frames of reference. We shall come back to this remark.

    6.   Let us now consider other links between meanings as they are shown in the research reported in the various chapters of this book. Here we should mention an important result: the early formation, at the level of actions, of operations which of course cannot be gathered yet in structured wholes (such as "groupings" for instance) but which, when considered separately and in their context of meanings, are isomorphic with respect to the 16 binary operations of propositional logic.

The importance of this finding is that it might be taken as contradicting everything that genetic psychology has been maintaining concerning the stage of "formal operations." In fact, it was explicitly said that the 16 binary operations of propositional logic characterized systems which are constructed at 11-12 years only. This classic assertion of genetic psychol-

---

[1]This distinction between proactive and retroactive implications happens to coincide with a distinction Peirce drew a long time ago. He called these two forms "predictive" and "retrodictive" implications.

ogy was based on two main reasons. The first reason was that hypothetical-deductive thinking—i.e., an ability to draw necessary consequences from mere hypotheses instead of relying on observable data (as at the level of "concrete operations," seven-ten years)—starts at this level only. The second reason for such a late formation was that the 16 binary operations are related through inversions N and reciprocities R which make up the quaternality groups ($INRC$ groups in which C is the reverse of R and the correlative of identity I) that the subject *uses* in physical situations (such as in the well-known case of the pendulum).

The findings of the 16 binary combinations at the level of coordinations among actions—that is, well before hypothetical-deductive thinking and *a fortiori* before the use of the $INRC$ structure—may be taken as being in flagrant contradiction with the above. This notwithstanding, the situation is quite different. We actually observe at early levels the 16 possible combinations of *pairs of actions*, but with no structured wholes. *Each combination is performed differently according to varying contexts.*

7. There is, therefore, a long process of *construction* of logical links which the subjects elaborate in various situations. Logical connectives acquire in this way various possible interpretations. There are several "and"s, several "or"s, and several forms of negations, differing as far as "intensions" are concerned, that the experiments described in the chapters of this book have attempted to identify. Thus, for instance, in the research on tiling described in chapter 3 on tiling it is clear that there are implications between actions, incompatibilities, and so on. The analysis shows that, in fact, the children are *using* about 11 of the 16 binary operations. Other experiments, described in other chapters, show other combinations including the remaining links. We have thus observed the early formation of intersections, incompatibilities, etc., which are used at the level of actions and not of statements. Once again, this shows the general formative role of the logic of actions and action implications, in which meaning implications that go far beyond extensional implications originate.

Each of these various initial links will form first separately, and then with others *fragments of structures* that will be gradually coordinated until "groupings" are constructed from seven-eight years on. These first structurations, which originate in interacting meanings, are interesting in that they do not only prepare the formation of groupings at the level of concrete operations, but also prepare the formation of the more complex operations of propositional logic.

8.   Let us now take up a few of the results concerning some logical connectives. In the case of the conjunction, the various studies have made it obvious that this kind of a link may present itself in several forms. There are, to start with, two kinds of conjunctions. Reference is made in the text to "constrained conjunctions" when p cannot be separated from q because they are part of the same nesting. On the other hand, the expression "free conjunction" is used when a link and a conjunction do not necessarily exist between the two terms.

It is clear that the above distinction starts already at very elementary levels. The simplest cases involve the meanings of predicates. They can be defined as the whole set of resemblances and differences between an observed property and the other simultaneously registered or already known predicates. Therefore predicates are linked through preoperations of conjunctions that can be, in Piaget's words, either "constrained" (i.e., necessary, with a mutual implication, as between shape and size) or "free" (i.e., contingent, as between shape and color). In between those two kinds of conjunctions, we have observed what Piaget called in chapter 4 "coupled predicates" which are linked through "pseudo-constrained" conjunctions. (In a seriation, for instance, it is as if the size of the middle element was modified through a change in positions.)

Similar distinctions are found in the text with reference to various kinds of disjunctions.

In the case of negation, there is an obvious distinction to be made between two different meanings already referred to above. In extensional logic, the reference frame for negation is the whole universe of speech, whereas some negations are relative to the closest nestings of a given statement.   For instance, in the classical extensional implication $p{\supset}q{\equiv}(p{\cdot}q{\vee}\bar{p}{\cdot}q{\vee}\bar{p}{\cdot}\bar{q})$, the statement $\bar{p}$ in $\bar{p}{\cdot}q$ or in $\bar{p}{\cdot}\bar{q}$ is everything that is not p and not the complementary of p under q. For instance, if class B includes subclasses A and A', then $B - A' = A$. Here the negation refers to class B as including both subclasses. Piaget speaks of a "proximal" negation as being relative to the closest nesting. On the other hand, he speaks of a "distal" negation when $\bar{p}$ is all that is not p in the universe of speech, independently of possible nestings.

Once these distinctions are accepted, we may notice that the binary operations include 16 cases, but that they are more numerous according to the kinds of conjunctions, negations and even disjunctions that were actually observed. Such varieties of operations depend on contexts and reference frames—i.e., on the nestings involved.

9. Two more remarks are needed in order to wind up the results. First, it is clear that there is no room here to make a sharp distinction between what Frege called *"Sinn"* (connotation) and *"Bedeutung"* (denotation). *Sinn* is meaning; *Bedeutung* its extension.[2] They can never be separated. They are two aspects of the same process, which essentially correspond to the two directions of the assimilation process identified by Piaget: an *attributive* assimilation going from a known scheme to a new object (in other words, when a new object is understood through a known scheme) and an *integrative* assimilation going from a new object to a scheme. The first kind of assimilation enriches the new object without necessarily modifying the scheme. In the case of an integrative assimilation, the subject knows what the new object means and recognizes what it is because the assimilation to a previous scheme is already known.

If we relate to the main claim of this book, according to which the psychogenetic roots of logic are found in meanings and in implications between them, an important consequence arises: as an object of knowledge, an object is nothing but a set of conjoined predicates, and its meaning amounts to "what can be done with it," i.e., to the assimilation to an action scheme (whether the action is a material one or a mental one). The dual direction of the process of assimilation shows that a logic of meanings, preceding and preparing the way to a logic of statements, has to proceed along the lines of both an intensional and an extensional logical theory (which originates in integrative assimilation).

The second remark concerns the great flexibility of a logical theory starting from inferences and taking the relation of meaning implication as the basic logical link. It should be emphasized time and time again that in the research reported in the chapters of this book, the logical connectives "intensionally" have various meanings according to the conjunctions, disjunctions, incompatibilities, mutual implications, etc., and that the subjects elaborate *on the basis of meaning implications,* which come down to combinations among implications and negations. We thus find a number of actual ways of dealing with "kinds" of disjunctions and conjunctions that correspond to the intensional logical connectives. This is the case of "cotenability," the intensional conjunction defined in the Introduction.

$$p \bigcirc q =_{Df} \overline{p \rightarrow \overline{q}}$$

[2] As the rest of this paragraph makes clear, in intensional logic, the extension of a meaning is quite different from the extension of a predicate or a proposition, which extensional logic takes as their referent. (J.E.)

10. We are now in a position to sum up the results and to place them within the wider context of the *Essai de logique opératoire* (LO).

The research that has been reported allows us to reformulate the central tenets of LO in three different directions, each of which requires, needless to say, further research efforts.

a) The main purpose of this book was to show how the construction of a logic of actions is prepared in childhood as a necessary substratum for operatory logic. In order to do that it was necessary to make a close analysis of meaning implications, especially those which consist of implications among actions or among operations. The concept of an action implication is the most original notion introduced in the book. To further analyze this form of implication one must go back as far as possible in psychogenetic evolution at the level of actions and the most elementary inferences.

b) The second objective of the research has been clearly attained. The aim was to show that at a very early stage, at the level of actions, one observes the early formation of operations each of which, when considered separately and *in its context of meanings*, is isomorphic with respect to one of the 16 binary operations of propositional logic.

c) The third objective was not only to show that logical connectives start long before the "operatory" stages, but rather that logical relations are constructed by fragments that gradually merge into logical structures.

As a final remark, let us recall, once more, the central thesis of genetic epistemology that forms the basis of the research reported in this book.

The knowing subjects, including the norms they themselves are always elaborating (without needing philosophers or psychologists to prescribe them), cannot be objectively understood at the beginning, at the end, nor at any stage in their history or formation because they are never completed systems. The subject's true nature lies in being a *self-organizing process*. This process is a continuous one and its general vection(s) alone has (have) an epistemological significance. The major problem is to reconstitute such vections, although they are never completed and can be grasped through reconstitution only, and never through *a priori* deduction. No amount of philosophical speculation, nor of rigorous logical analyses, may substitute for it.

Author Index

Subject Index

A

A priori , 127
Abstractions,
    Empirical, 39
    Reflective, 39, 89, 139, 161
Action implications, vii, 8, 9, 13,
    19, 31, 36, 38, 53, 89, 107-
    108, 120-121, 160-163, 166
Actions,
    Causality of, vii
    Coordinations of, 28, 89
    Meaning of, vii, 160
    Transforming, 131
Activities, spontaneous, 105
Algebra, Genetic, 138, 140
Algorithm, Growth, 136
Anticipations, 44, 160-161
    Inferential, 17
    Partial, 37
Assertion, Restricted, 149
Assimilation, 4
    Attributive, 165
    Integrative, 165
    Process of, 165
Associativity, 132
Atom, 150
Attribution of,
    Actions, 13
    Assimilation schemes, 159

B

Behavior, Instrumental, 9
Biology, 125-126
Boa constrictor, 58, 66
Box, 9, 44
Burali-Forti Paradox, 143-144

C

Calculation, 53
Calculus,
    Extensional, 151
    Truth-functional, 151
    Propositional, 156-157
Candles, 96
Cantor's Paradox, 144
Centrations, 22, 108
Chaining, Simple, 108
Classification, 111, 131
    Encompassing, 108
    Hierarchized, 108
    Infralogical, 22
    Of variable elements, 95
    Operational, 26
Classification grouping, 19, 21
Collections, 70
Combinations, 134
Commutability, 132
Commutativity, 132